The Way of Healing

The Way

of

Healing

Compiled by Lyn Klug

A LION BOOK

This edition copyright © 1999 Lion Publishing

Published by
Lion Publishing plc
Sandy Lane West, Oxford, England
www.lion-publishing.co.uk
ISBN 0 7459 4210 5

First published in America in 1998
as *All Will Be Well: A gathering of healing prayers*
by Augsburg Fortress, P.O. Box 1209
Minneapolis, MN 55440-1209

First UK edition 1999
10 9 8 7 6 5 4 3 2 1 0

A catalogue record for this book is available
from the British Library

Typeset in 12/14 Venetian 301
Printed and bound in Great Britain by
Biddles Ltd, Guildford and King's Lynn

Contents

Introduction

For thousands of years, people have looked to God for healing and wholeness. Today, there is a new openness to spiritual healing expressed by doctors, psychologists and those who suffer. While we are grateful for all the life-giving scientific advances in medicine, we know there are ways of healing that are beyond the reach of science. Healing remains a mystery involving our minds, souls, relationships, personal histories, the communities in which we live and the earth itself.

When we or our loved ones experience illness – in body, mind or spirit – our resources are stretched to the utmost. We struggle with feelings of fear, anxiety, helplessness and desperation. We do what we can, but often it is just not enough. We need help from beyond ourselves.

At times prayer comes to us spontaneously. We find it easy to turn in faith to a loving God, expressing in our own words what is on our hearts and minds. But at other times we are overcome by fatigue, stress, doubts and confusion. The words will not come. At times like this we can turn to those who have gone before us on the road of suffering. Those who have written about their healings have left us words that can speak for us, helping us express what is otherwise inexpressible, renewing our trust in God the Healer and showing us that we are not alone, no matter what we may be feeling.

Trust is not easy. The prayers of many great believers include cries of pain, despair and doubt. But those who have been honest to God in their worst moments allow us to be honest in ours, opening the way for healing. Some wise prayers enable us to see things from a new

perspective, others to give thanks for the good that
is present even in the midst of pain. Most important,
other people's prayers move us into our own. We speak
our true thoughts and feelings. We listen; some prayers
become a word from God to us. Best of all may be the
times when these words lead us to rest silently in the
presence of God.

Prayer, whether written or flowing freely from the
heart, releases the healing power of God into our situation.
The results of our prayer may not always correspond to
our wishes, but we trust that God's gift to us is always
love, God's desire is always what is best for us and our
loved ones, God's vision is always wider and wiser than
our own. We anchor our faith on the hope that in God's
good time and in God's way, all will be well.

How to use this book

Books of written prayers can be used in many ways,
whether you are praying for yourself or for a friend or
family member. The Spirit of God will lead you to use
this book in ways that are most beneficial for you. Here
are some ways to begin:

❙ Read the book through or browse the sections that
  attract you, stopping to reflect on those prayers that
  connect with your experience.

❙ Use the prayers you need at this time, and let the
  others be. At some time in the future, those prayers
  may become yours as well.

❙ Adapt the prayers to your own life situation or that
  of your loved ones.

❙ Respond to the prayers in a journal, beginning an

ongoing dialogue with God that can renew your spirit and help you make good choices in difficult times.

▌ Share the prayers with those you love and those for whom you pray. Include prayers in letters you write or leave them at the bedside of those you visit.

▌ Use the book as a resource for a prayer circle, healing ministry or spirituality group.

Because each of us is a unique person at a particular place in our spiritual journey, we must find our own ways to pray, but we trust that the Spirit of God leads us in that search. When we are in great need, we seek until we find what truly helps us, and God sends blessings we never could have found on our own. Books like this can be our companions in the search for healing.

May God be with us as we seek healing for ourselves, our loved ones and the world.

Let Comfort Come

Prayers for physical healing

Almighty God, you are the source of health and healing,
the spirit of calm, and the central peace of the universe.
We ask that you would fill us with such an awareness of
your presence within that we may have complete confidence
in you. In all pain and weariness and anxiety may we rest
in your protecting care; may we know ourselves to be
encircled by your loving power so that we may allow you
to give us health and strength and peace, through Jesus
Christ, our Lord. Amen.

AVERY BROOKE

Merciful God,
Loving Mother,
Guiding Light.
Let comfort come this night
   for every wound and distress
   for every sorrow and uncertainty:
Your love shines upon us;
Your love will guard our rest.

DANIEL J. McGILL

Just for today,
What does it matter, O Lord, if the future is dark?
To pray now for tomorrow – I am not able.
Keep my heart only for today,
   give me your protection today,
   grant me your light –
   just for today.

ST THÉRÈSE OF LISIEUX (1873–97)

From moment to moment one can bear much.

ST TERESA OF AVILA (1515–82)

My God – equally present
In darkness as in light,
Stand by me!
Allow me, yes, to suffer and be hurt,
But not to be broken or destroyed.
Allow me to be bruised,
But not my spirit to be overcome.
I know of suffering and I do not fear it.
I only fear my strength to carry it.
I ask not to escape from the threats and the pain,
I ask that I might carry them
With grace,
With hope,
With love.

EDWINA GATELEY

Help me to be brave.
Help me to be hopeful.
Help me to face cheerfully and openly – rather than
reluctantly and resentfully – whatever is coming next,
wherever it is that I am going.

JOAN BEL GEDDES

Praying a Bible text

Repeated slowly many times, then silently many times,
allowing the meaning to deepen into feeling, holding
the attention on the text whenever it strays away, until
at last the mind is silent and I experience the truth of
the promise of which the text speaks.

Peace I leave with you, my peace I give unto you.

It is I, be not afraid.

11

Abide in me and let me abide in you.

Underneath are the everlasting arms.

I am with you always.

In quietness and confidence shall be your strength.

I have made, and I will bear.

Your ears shall hear a word behind you, saying,
this is the way, walk in it.

I will never leave you nor forsake you.

GEORGE APPLETON (1902–93)

Jesus,
you wasted no time agonizing over
the great wound of pain and suffering in creation,
or in asking who dealt this wound.
You simply accepted it as the mystery of existence
and then devoted your life to healing it.
The crowd read in your eyes God's love
for them in their miserable condition
and flocked to you. The crowd laid bare
its painful, suffering wound,
and you touched the wound with your hand,
your most personal human hand –
and healed it.

No gospel of suffering in the Gospels, then –
just you – God's Yes to a suffering world.
No illumination of pain and suffering in the Gospels –
just you, God's I Am Love,
radiantly and utterly illuminated.

EDNA HONG

Some people find the imagination a useful tool in prayer. Picture Jesus healing people, and then see him walking towards you, looking at you with deep compassion, and stretching out his hands towards you. You could imagine that Jesus takes both your hands in his. Feel the warmth; the love; the sense of security, come what may. There is a Celtic encircling prayer which you could say as you imagine this:

> I place my hands in yours, Lord,
> I place my hands in yours.
> I place my will in yours, Lord,
> I place my will in yours.
> I place my days in yours, Lord,
> I place my days in yours.
> I place my thoughts in yours, Lord,
> I place my thoughts in yours.
> I place my heart in yours, Lord,
> I place my heart in yours.
> I place my hands in yours, Lord,
> I place my hands in yours.
>
> ANGELA ASHWIN

I experienced it again today.
You were suddenly there
with your surprising presence.

You were suddenly there
without any visible reason,
without my having done anything,
without preparation,
without warning.
Suddenly you were there
with your complete joy,

with the relaxation which emanates from you,
with the sense you put back into life.

There you are
and I can only smile
at how connected everything is in my life.

Ulrich Schaffer

We cannot fall beneath the arms of God.
However low we fall,
they are still underneath us.

William Penn (1644–1718)

Dear God,
The pain of this life is more than I can bear.
I feel as though death would be better.
My thoughts are dark, my sorrows huge.
I feel as though I shall not endure, and there is
   no one and nothing to turn to now.
My hurt is so big.
I cannot handle this.
If you can, dear God, please do.
If you can, please do. Amen.

Marianne Williamson

Jesus Christ, if you had not cried
'My God, my God,
Why hast thou forsaken me?'
I would be an atheist.

Thomas R. Heath OP

Help of the tired ones,
I am in need tonight –
so weary I can hardly think

or pray aright;
but you have known the toil,
the grief, the strain
of human suffering,
and felt the pain
of utter weariness —
the sting of tears, fatigue —
and so you know my need.

I have no words to say,
but in my heart
I pray.

MARY ESTHER BURGOYNE

May the God who listens to our hearts and enters into
our pain bless us and all who are in need with the comfort
and quiet of her gentle presence, now and always. Amen.

MARCHIENE VROON RIENSTRA

Dear Lord, in the midst of much inner turmoil and
restlessness, there is a consoling thought: maybe you are
working in me in a way I cannot yet feel, experience or
understand. My mind is not able to concentrate on you,
my heart is not able to remain centred, and it seems as
if you are absent and have left me alone. But in faith
I cling to you. I believe that your Spirit reaches deeper
and further than my mind or heart, and that profound
movements are not the first to be noticed.

Therefore, Lord, I promise I will not run away, not
give up, not stop praying, even when it all seems useless,
pointless and a waste of time and effort. I want to let
you know that I love you even though I do not feel
loved by you, and that I hope in you even though I often
experience despair. Let this be a little dying I can do with

you and for you as a way of experiencing some solidarity with the millions in this world who suffer far more than I do. Amen.

HENRI NOUWEN (1932–96)

Almighty God, whose most dear Son went not up to joy but first he suffered pain, and entered not into glory before he was crucified: mercifully grant that we, walking in the way of the cross, may find it none other than the way of life and peace; through Jesus Christ your Son our Lord, who lives and reigns with you and the Holy Spirit, one God, for ever and ever. Amen.

THE BOOK OF COMMON PRAYER

Lord, let me make sickness itself a prayer.

ST FRANCIS OF SALES (1567–1622)

O Lord, it has been a while since I've walked on grass or seen the stars in the sky. So many silent and restless nights, so many long and boring days in a hospital bed. At first I was too sick to care, but now I am getting impatient to go home. I get upset about my dependency, my setbacks, my slow progress. At times even the people who are trying to do their best to help me irritate me and get on my nerves. It's not really their fault. It's just me, that I can only take so much and then I have to let it out. But since, O Lord, you have taken me this far, since you have given me enough patience to endure, I pray again that you heal that which still needs to be healed in me. May I soon breathe fresh air and enjoy the atmosphere of my own home. I ask this in Jesus' name. Amen.

FATHER ARNALDO PANGRAZZI

Thank you, O God, for all the people who have looked after me today… Into your strong hands I place all the patients in this ward…
the night staff on duty tonight…
my loved ones whose names I now mention…
myself, with my fears, my worries and my hopes…
Help me to sleep, thinking of you and your promises.
Amen.

CHRISTIAN PUBLICITY ORGANIZATION

Bless her for not saying, 'you look terrific;'
(I would have to fib back, 'I feel pretty good, too.')
Bless her for not talking about *her* aches and pains;
(I sense they are probably more painful than mine.)
Bless her for her smile that lights up my room;
(One of those genuine smiles that are so rare today.)
But most of all, God, bless this dear thoughtful soul
for sneaking me a corned beef on rye.

JOHN V. CHERVOKAS

They don't call.
They don't come.
I feel invisible, forgotten.
I know they are busy.
I've been busy myself.
But… it means so much.
Maybe they don't realize it,
as I didn't, back when…
But, right now,
I feel forgotten
by those I love most.
Empty, when I'd rather be full,
is how I come to you this day, my God.

MARLENE HALPIN

Breathing deeply and slowly, silently say part of a line as you inhale, and part as you exhale. As the prayer is repeated, painful areas in the body relax and God's peace is received into the deep levels of the mind.

The Lord is my shepherd. I shall not want.

O Lord, make haste to help me.

Jesus, Healer, make me whole.

I'm afraid, Lord. I need you.

Please give me the strength I need.

Whatever will heal me, please send it now.

Holy Spirit, breathe in me.

> Christ be with me, Christ within me,
> Christ behind me, Christ before me,
> Christ beside me, Christ to win me,
> Christ to comfort and restore me.

Jesus breathed on them, and said to them, 'Receive the Holy Spirit.'

JOHN 20:22

Let everything that breathes praise the Lord!

PSALM 150:6

Gently and lightly massage the hands, face and neck. Claim with trust the presence of Jesus Christ, the incarnate love of God, always with you. Relax your body, close your eyes and picture around you some light, colour, water, warmth, breeze or other symbol of God's energizing and enfolding presence.

Listen to any signals from the body of physical discomfort, pain, tension, unease. Focus on that part of your body, feeling it breathing in and out as if that part had its own separate breathing apparatus. Let that body part breathe slowly for several minutes. Visualize God's surrounding light or breath flowing in and out of that area.

When it feels right, move on to another area, letting that area breathe in and out. This is a powerful pain reliever. Now let your whole body breathe slowly, gently, from the soles of the feet to the top of the head. Don't gasp or push it.

Now just sit quietly, leaning on the strength of God, letting God's life-giving breath flow in and out of your body. Give thanks, and, when ready, open your eyes.

FLORA SLOSSON WUELLNER

All is ill and very ill
but all will be well again.
Time will heal,
time will mend.
All will be well again!

EDNA HONG

And so our Good Lord answered to all the questions and doubts which I could raise, saying most comfortingly: I may make all things well, and I can make all things well, and I shall make all things well... And you will see yourself that every kind of thing will be well... And in these... words, God wishes us to be enclosed in rest and in peace.

JULIAN OF NORWICH (1342–1419)

'That which is impossible for you is not impossible
    to me:
I will preserve my word in all things and I will make
    all things well.'

This is the great deed that our God will do.

Our faith is grounded in God's Word and we must let
    this trust be.
How it will be done we will not know until it is done,
because God wants us to be at ease and at peace,
not troubled or kept from enjoying God.

God does not want us to be burdened because of
    sorrows and tempests that happen in our lives,
because it has always been so before miracles happen.

JULIAN OF NORWICH (1342–1419)

Once life has almost been taken from you,
when for some strange reason
you emerge from death
and blink with new eyes
upon the old, almost forgotten universe,
then you can understand once more
the value of sea and stars,
of happiness uncontainable,
the sheer relief and delight of being alive
that turns your eyes repeatedly upwards
with thanksgiving,
then straight outward
declaring peace over and over again
to those who with heads bent low
see mud, not stars.

KATHY KEAY (1954–94)

May the Light shine on all your days.
It is there, despite illness, defeat and tears.
It is eternal.

HARVEY STOWER

The Burdens We Carry

Prayers for mental and emotional healing

God of our life,
there are days when the burdens we carry
chafe our shoulders and weigh us down;
when the road seems dreary and endless,
the skies grey and threatening;
when our lives have no music in them,
and our hearts are lonely,
and our souls have lost their courage.

Flood the path with light, we beseech thee;
turn our eyes to where the skies are full of promise;
tune our hearts to brave music;
give us the sense of comradeship with heroes and
    saints of every age;
and so quicken our spirits that we may be able to
    encourage
the souls of all who journey with us on the road to life,
to thy honour and glory.

ST AUGUSTINE OF HIPPO (354–430)

I am, O God, a jumbled mass of motives; one moment
I am adoring you, and the next I am shaking my fist at
you. I vacillate between mounting hope and deepening
despair. I am full of faith, and full of doubt. I want the
best for others, and am jealous when they get it. Even
so, God, I will not run from your presence. Nor will I
pretend to be what I am not. Thank you for accepting
me with all my contradictions. Amen.

RICHARD J. FOSTER

O God, Giver of Life, Bearer of Pain, Maker of Love,
you are able to accept in us what we
cannot even acknowledge;
you are able to name in us what we
cannot bear to speak of;
you are able to hold in your memory
what we have tried to forget;
you are able to hold out to us
the glory that we cannot conceive of.
Reconcile us through your cross
to all that we have rejected in our selves,
that we may find no part of your creation
to be alien or strange to us,
and that we ourselves may be made whole.
Through Jesus Christ, our lover and our friend. Amen.

JANET MORLEY

I keep projecting my present condition onto the future.
If I feel dark, the future looks dark; if I feel bright, the
future looks bright. But who am I to know what life will
be like for me tomorrow, next week, next year or ten
years from now? Even more, who am I to know who you
will be for me in the year ahead? O Lord, I will not bind
you with my own limited and limiting ideas and feelings.
You can do so many things with me, things that might
seem totally impossible to me. I want at least to remain
open to the free movement of your Spirit in my life.
Why do I keep saying to myself: 'I will never be a saint.
I will never be able to overcome my impulses and desires.'
If I keep saying that, I might prevent you from healing
and touching me deeply. O Lord, let me remain free to
let you come whenever and however you desire. Amen.

HENRI NOUWEN (1932–96)

O Love unspeakable and full of glory, whose majesty is not to destroy, but to save, save us from ourselves. Our past relentlessly pursues us. Days that we thought dead live over again; deeds that we deemed buried meet us on the way; be thou our defence, O our God.

Fill up that which our lives have left behind. Undo that which we have done amiss. Repair the places we have wasted, bind the hearts we have wounded. Dry the eyes which we have flooded. Make the evil we have done work for good, so that we ourselves would not know it.

Take up our yesterdays into thine own golden light and transfigure them there, that we may learn with joyful surprise how even against our wills we were labouring together with thee; so shall our former selves find us no more. Amen.

AUTHOR UNKNOWN

Give me a candle of the Spirit, O God, as I go down into the deeps of my being. Show me the hidden things, the creatures of my dreams, the storehouse of forgotten memories and hurts. Take me down to the spring of my life and tell me my nature and my name. Give me freedom to grow, so that I may become that self, the seed of which you planted in me at my making. Out of the deeps I cry to you, O God.

GEORGE APPLETON (1902–93)

I carry the sorrows
of my years
within me.
Often,
not even loved ones
know.

Some burdens
have gotten lighter
with time.

Others
weigh heavier still.

I give my secret pain
to you, God.
Help me!

Pat Corrick Hinton

Now you too may kneel before the Christ child to leave at his feet those unseen, secret things that may be left nowhere else but there. And having visited the holy place, you too, like those three visitors of old, may go on your way made new.

Paul Flucke

This life is not a state of being righteous,
but rather, of growth in righteousness;
not a state of being healthy, but a period of healing;
not a state of being, but becoming;
not a state of rest, but of exercise and activity.
We are not yet what we shall be, but we grow towards it;
the process is not yet finished, but is still going on;
this life is not the end, it is the way to a better.
All does not yet shine with glory;
nevertheless, all is being purified.*

Martin Luther (1483–1546)

* 2 Corinthians 3:18

Holy Spirit,
giving life to all life,
moving all creatures,
root of all things,
washing them clean,
wiping out their mistakes,
healing their wounds,
you are our true life,
luminous, wonderful,
awakening the heart
from its ancient sleep.

HILDEGARD OF BINGEN (1098–1179),
TRANSLATED BY STEPHEN MITCHELL

When I was small the words would not come.
I could not speak.
The people looked at me and asked about me
and wondered about me,
but I couldn't speak.
I was silent, and they shook their heads and walked away.
Now I am grown, and words come.
I speak.
The people look at me and ask about me
and wonder about me still, and I speak.
I say, 'Yes, children do get hurt.' I say, 'No, I don't
    understand.'
I say, 'child sexual abuse'. I say, 'incest'. I say, 'pain'.
Then they look beyond me and long to be gone,
away from my painful truths.
They shake their heads and walk away.
But you, Jesus, you tell stories of people who listened.
You tell stories of those who stopped and stooped
to hear the pain.

Samaritans, approaching the wounded.
Willing to feel pain as they listen to pain.
You tell stories of seeing, of hearing, of neighbours,
 of love.
And you, Jesus. You say, 'Tell me.'
You say, 'Speak. I am not afraid to feel.'
You approach the pain.
You teach me that pain will not destroy.
When the storm is over, the resurrection begins.

CATHERINE J. FOOTE

Dear God,
I feel such pain, anxiety and depression.
I know this is not your will for me,
and yet my mind is held in chains by fear and paranoia.
I surrender my life, right now, to you.
Take the entire mess, all of it,
now too complicated to explain to anyone
but known by you in each detail.
Do what I cannot do.
Lift me up.
Give me a new chance.
Show me a new light.
Make me a new person.
Dear God,
This depression frightens me.
Dear God,
Please bring me peace. Amen.

MARIANNE WILLIAMSON

I was terrified I'd break down.
I did.
It didn't matter.

ROSALIND M. BAKER

Dear Higher Power,
Show me the Miracle of your Love in this situation,
because I only see resentment and hatred.
Show me the Miracle of your Healing,
because I cannot stop seeing what is diseased.
Give me the Miracle of your Release,
because I am afraid to let go.
Bring me the Miracle of your Faith,
because I am overwhelmed by doubt and confusion.
Show me the Light of your Care,
because I feel alone and lost in darkness.
Show me the Miracle of your Vision,
for I see myself and others with eyes
of judgment and quiet condemnation.
Show me the Miracle of Life,
because I have been fighting and do not trust it.
Be the Miracle in my life. Amen.

GERALDINE MOSLEY

Lord,
first let us hear the voice
crying in the wilderness of our own hearts.

ADAPTED FROM GEORGE FOX (1624–91)

God, I just want to talk to you, I just want to open my
soul to you. I don't want to try to say it right. I don't
want to meet someone else's expectations of what I should
say or what I should believe. I just want to talk to you.

I sit sometimes in a deep well. I can't get out. I'm so
tired of the struggle. I ache. I want to stop time and spend
time with me. But time moves on and takes me with it.

God, I'm too tired to hold on, and I don't know any
way out. This aching human part of me, what do I do

with this? God, you have abandoned me. I cannot pretend
that I feel you here. I cannot pretend that I'm OK. All
I can do is hold on and hope this feeling will pass. All I
can do is trust that it will stop and when I pass through,
you will be there on the other side. Amen.

CATHERINE J. FOOTE

Go, and know that the Lord goes with you: let him lead
you each day into the quiet place of your heart, where he
will speak with you; know that he loves you and watches
over you – that he listens to you in gentle understanding,
that he is with you always, wherever you are and however
you may feel: and the blessings of God – Father, Son and
Holy Spirit – be yours for ever.

AUTHOR UNKNOWN

Who can boast of being free?
Who has not got secret prisons,
invisible chains, all the more constricting
the less they are apparent?

DOM HELDER CAMARA

Lord,
free us from falling into the sin
of believing that the slavery in Egypt
is better than the struggles in the desert.

TÓMAS H. TÉLLEZ

Well, my poor heart, here we are,
fallen into the ditch which we
had made so firm a resolution to avoid;
oh! let us rise and leave it for ever.
Courage! Henceforth, let us be more on our guard.
God will help us, we shall do well enough!

ST FRANCIS OF SALES (1567–1622)

Take my weakness, God.
Take my failures, my sins, my dishonesties,
lies, pride and lusts.
God knows – you know –
I can't do anything with them.
So, for Christ's sake, take them.
And give me, I pray you,
not so much a clean spirit,
nor a pure heart,
nor a sense of forgiveness –
give me a sense of you,
of you in me, and I in you.
Then shall I be strong to be for you.
Simply to be.

JOHN B. COBURN

God, whose name is Truth –
I thirst for honesty, integrity, sincerity.
There are lies here.
There are opaque places in my spirit.
There are delusions, chains, deceptions, clouds.
Give me the grace to let these shadows go,
to find your Truth already hidden in my heart.

HOLLY JO TURNQUIST FISCHER

Dear God, I feel that I have wasted my life, thrown
away my resources, taken too much time to gather my
strengths. Now, dear God, I feel it is too late for me.
My age, my weaknesses, the lies and betrayals of time
gone by, all make me seem a lesser talent. And only
you, dear God, know the love in my heart and how
much I want to serve, how much I have to give. I need
a miracle, a new beginning, which only you can give me.

Please, dear God, I give my life to you. Please bring together my talents. Please increase my gifts and use them for your purposes. I surrender my future. Make it unlike my past. Thank you very much. Amen.

MARIANNE WILLIAMSON

My mind is happy today in the thought that I am God's child in God's world to do God's work within God's will.

This is to be a day of joy and optimism and courage. From all negative thoughts my mind resolutely turns away.

The Spirit of God is working in my body to bring health, and in my mind to bring serenity, and I am one with that Spirit. I am not apart from, or disapproved of, or turned away by, God. No impostor-fears shall let me think I am.

I affirm the reality of health and peace and love within me because God dwells therein.

LESLIE WEATHERHEAD (1883–1975)

Dear God: Help me to admit mistakes freely without feeling shame, and to recognize that they come to teach me. Help me to find my own voice, to say what I mean and mean what I say. Help me to see the good and to laugh at myself and at life more. Help me to discover my gifts and honour the uniqueness of others. Help me to accept who I am, a beloved and special being in your eyes. And above all, help me to remain patient and gentle with myself.

ROBERT AND JANET ELLSWORTH

As swimmers dare
to lie face to the sky
and water bears them,
as hawks rest upon air
and air sustains them,
so would I learn to attain
free fall, and float
into Creator Spirit's deep embrace,
knowing no effort earns
that all-surrounding grace.

DENISE LEVERTOV (1923–97)

Sometimes
I go about pitying myself
While I am carried by
The wind
Across the sky.

CHIPPEWA SONG

O Lord, please send me someone who can take the time to notice me, someone who can visit me to break the silence of my day, someone who can put her hands into my heart and draw out into the light my inner longings, someone who can listen with their eyes and hear my hunger, someone who can smile at me, someone who can reflect with me. Someone, I am lonely for you today. Why do you run away from me? Is time too short for you to love? What do you see in me that scares you?

Remember, Someone, that if you take time to hear my silence, I will take time to unfold my presence; if you take time to touch my pain, I will take time to give you purpose; if you take time to accept my seasons, I will take time to change your heart.

Someone, don't be afraid about what to say, just stay with me and hold my hand. Tomorrow I might not pass this way again. Amen.

FATHER ARNALDO PANGRAZZI

Dear Lord Jesus,
I don't know who I am,
I don't know where I am,
and I don't know what I am,
but please love me.

SUFFERER FROM ALZHEIMER'S DISEASE

Breath prayers for inner healing can be prayed anywhere, any time, especially when we are distressed or discouraged. Slow, deep breathing calms the mind and body, and the prayer turns us towards God.

Out of the depths have I cried unto thee, O Lord. Lord, hear my voice.

Where the Spirit of the Lord is, there is freedom.

Lord of life, send my roots rain.

I love you, O Lord, my strength.

Show me, O Lord, the path of life.

You can also pray while you work. Work doesn't stop prayer, and prayer doesn't stop work. It requires only that small raising of the mind to God. 'I love you, God, I trust you, I believe in you, I need you now,' small things like that. They are wonderful prayers.

MOTHER TERESA OF CALCUTTA (1910–97)

When I come to the end of my prayers, I find that
there are prayers I still need.
A prayer for the courage to speak the truth.
Another prayer for the pain.
A prayer for the sadness.
A prayer for fears.
A prayer for the anger that sometimes smoulders
and sometimes burns.
A prayer for justice and for grace.
A prayer for strength to keep telling my story,
to keep moving towards wholeness, to keep moving
towards you.
A prayer for wisdom.
Another prayer for love. Amen.

CATHERINE J. FOOTE

Thy Kingdom Come

Prayers for the healing of community

Thy kingdom come,
Thy will be done,
On earth as it is in heaven.

MATTHEW 6:10

O Lord, whose power to heal was tested against the power which destroys, and proved stronger: open our eyes to the signs of your strength in this modern world, and open our hearts to the Kingdom of God, which has come upon us; through the power of your Spirit. Amen.

SUSAN WILLIAMS

Bless your people, Lord,
who have walked too long in this night of pain.
For the child has no more tears to cry
and the old people no song of joy to sing,
and the blood of our youth drains away in the gutters.
The cry from the cross is heard throughout the land.
The pain in your nailed hands is carried by the worker.
Terrible thirst is in the mouth of the farmer,
too many women mourn the loss of their sons,
and all the earth is turned into another Calvary.
With your spirit, Lord, we cry for peace.
With your spirit, we struggle to be free.

NATIONAL COUNCIL OF CHURCHES OF THE PHILIPPINES

Lord Jesus, you were awakened by the cry of your disciples on a storm-tossed sea. Hear also our cry for help. There is no justice in our land for the weak and powerless, because the powerful and the strong have decided what is and what is not right and just. We, the minority of the humble and meek, are tired of crying for justice and peace. How much longer must the mighty dominate and the weak suffer? Bring your justice, and grant us your peace. Let your kingdom become a reality on this earth.

SRI LANKAN PRAYER

From the mingled light and shadow of hope
I greet you, Lord, God.

DOM HELDER CAMARA

Lord Jesus Christ, help us not to fall in love with the night that covers us but through the darkness to watch for you as well as to work for you; to dream and hunger in the dark for the light of you. Help us to know that the madness of God is saner than men…

Give us back the great hope again that the future is yours, that not even the world can hide you from us for ever, that at the end the One who came will come back in power to work joy in us stronger even than death. Amen.

FREDERICK BUECHNER

All the broken hearts shall rejoice;
all those who are heavy laden,
whose eyes are tired and do not see,
shall be lifted up
to meet with the motherly healer.
The battered souls and bodies shall be healed;
the hungry shall be fed;
the imprisoned shall be free;
all her earthly children shall regain joy
in the reign of the just and loving one
coming for you
coming for me
in this time
in this world.

SUN AI LEE PARK

I believe that God
has the whole world
in his hands.

He is not a bystander
at the pain of the world.
He does not stand
like Peter,
wringing his hands
in the shadows,
but is there,
in the dock,
on the rack,
high on the gallows tree.

He is *in* the pain
of the lunatic,
the tortured,
those wracked by grief.
His is the blood
that flows in the gutter.
His are the veins burned by heroin,
his the lungs choked by AIDS.
His is the heart
broken by suffering,
his the despair
of the mute,
the oppressed,
the man with the gun to his head.
He is the God of Paradox.

Sheila Cassidy

God of all good life, on our journey towards Easter, cleanse our hearts of every desire to mimic the violence of wrongs that befall us. Save us from becoming the evil we hate. Save us from denial of abuses which daily crucify Christ afresh. Drive away the chilling cold, the wintry frost, of numbing detachment from others' pain, and our own hurts, also. Breathe, O breathe your empowering Spirit into the troubled hearts of your children who wish they could wish to love but cannot.

Hear our prayer, in the name of Jesus, the Shining Way, the Truth and the Life. Amen.

OBIE WRIGHT JR

Oh Lord, once I was smart enough to know a just war when I saw it, the kind of war you would approve of. I am not so smart any more. Every war looks evil to me now. And even the war well begun becomes evil before it's over. So let us have no more of just wars; they are the worst kind. Now, at last, give us a just peace. It's time, Lord.

Past time. Time for Shalom. Shalom for our breaking hearts. It's time.

LEWIS B. SMEDES

Lead me from death to life, from falsehood to truth.
Lead me from despair to hope, from fear to trust.
Lead me from hate to love, from war to peace.
Let peace fill our heart, our world, our universe.
Peace. Peace. Peace.

SATISH KUMAR

Make that possible to us, O Lord, by grace, which appears impossible to us by nature.

THOMAS À KEMPIS (C. 1380–1471)

Goodness is stronger than evil;
Love is stronger than hate;
Light is stronger than darkness;
Life is stronger than death;
Victory is ours through him who loves us.

DESMOND TUTU

Bless, O God, my enemies with sunshine.
Upon their crops come shining.
May green grass grow in their meadows,
Sweet crops within their fields;
Send rain upon their soil,
Fill their children with joy,
Bless their grandparents with peace.
May every woman of them know delight;
May every man of them be loved.
May the birds of their air never hear bombs;
May their rivers run clean,
    their air smell sweet in the morning.

May all things with life be blessed!
For if my enemy is not blessed,
How can I, O Lord, be blessed?
How can I?
For earth shall cry if they shall weep,
And I shall cry if she is hurt.

DANIEL J. MCGILL

May those who sow in tears
    reap with shouts of joy!

PSALM 126:5

Almighty God and Father of us all,
Have mercy upon this troubled world of ours.
We are a pilgrim people, made of clay,
Captives of our own greed and frailty.
And yet, we are the work of your hands.
You have made us in your own image
And we bear within us
Your Spirit of life,
The seeds of immortality.
Give us, we pray,
A stronger faith
So that we may walk joyously into the unknown,
An unshakeable hope
So that we may comfort the despairing,
And a love
As vast as all the oceans
So that we may hold all humankind
In our hearts.
All-powerful God,
Look in your love upon us, your pilgrim people,
As we struggle towards you.
Be our food for the journey,
Our wine for rejoicing,
Our light in the darkness,
And our welcome at the journey's end.

SHEILA CASSIDY

Source of all life,
For your name's sake,
For your joy cast upon the earth,
For life's great delight in your handiwork,
Remember all the wounded and broken things,

unclean water
poisoned air
desecrated land
fleeing wildlife
dying innocents
And please remember us,
When our lives become enemies of your life.
Open our hearts to your family,
Earth's many children;
Return our hearts to you. Amen.

DANIEL J. MCGILL

O come, thou Dayspring, come and cheer
Our spirits by thine advent here;
Disperse the gloomy clouds of night,
And death's dark shadows put to flight.
Rejoice! Rejoice!
Emmanuel shall come to thee, O Israel!

O come, Desire of nations, bind
All peoples in one heart and mind;
Bid thou our sad divisions cease;
Fill the whole world with heaven's peace.
Rejoice! Rejoice!
Emmanuel shall come to thee, O Israel!

O come, thou Wisdom from on high,
Who ord'rest all things mightily;
To us the path of knowledge show
And teach us in her ways to go.
Rejoice! Rejoice!
Emmanuel shall come to thee, O Israel!

TRANSLATED FROM LATIN BY JOHN MASON NEALE (1818–66)

Put your ear to the ground
and listen:
hurried, worried footsteps,
bitterness, rebellion.
Hope
hasn't yet begun.
Listen again.
Put out feelers.
The Lord is there.
He is far less likely
to abandon us
in hardship
than in times of ease.

DOM HELDER CAMARA

*A Great
Emptiness*

Prayers for the healing of grief

Lament: Psalm 48

I am depressed, O God.
I see no end to this cycle of sadness.
People tell me: 'Everything will be all right,'
but it isn't, and it won't be.
They quote Paul to me:
'All things work together for good for those who
    love God.'
Don't I love you?
Wasn't I brought up in your holy house,
O God?
Didn't I memorize your words and sing hymns to you?
Don't I bow down to you?
Isn't that what I'm doing now?
No one can tell me any good can come from this
    moment!
Let them have their say if it makes them feel better!
But I don't want to hear it!
I know what I've been through.
I know what it is to have death walk the halls of
    my home.
What has happened can't be undone.
What is done cannot be prettied up.
But you, O God, can stop the aftershocks.
O God, tear through the night
to rescue the one you have left too long.
Help me, O Holy God,
out of this tomb of pain.

ANN WEEMS

How is faith to endure, O God, when you allow all this scraping and tearing on us? You have allowed rivers of blood to flow, mountains of suffering to pile up, sobs to become humanity's song – all without lifting a finger that we could see. You have allowed bonds of love beyond number to be painfully snapped. If you have not abandoned us, explain yourself.

We strain to hear. But instead of hearing an answer we catch sight of God himself scraped and torn. Through our tears we see the tears of God.

A new and more disturbing question now arises: Why do you permit yourself to suffer, O God? If the death of the devout costs you dear, why do you permit it? Why do you not grasp joy?

NICHOLAS WOLTERSTORFF

I believe in you,
O Holy One,
although at times
there no longer seems
any reason for believing.
When evil stalks
my dwelling place
and loneliness leaves
indelible traces of doubt
on my childhood faith,
I light a lamp
in the secret room
where my heart hides
its tradition
and quietly hug
your promises
as I sing songs to you.

I believe in you.
Believe in me.
May we believe for ever. Amen.

MIRIAM THERESE WINTER

50

There's not much to come home to
Now that she's gone.
I keep forgetting,
Sort of expecting her to be there
Like always.
So when I open the door
The silence hits me
Like a fist,
Knocks the wind out of me.
I'm glad there's nobody there to see.
They'd send me up like a kook.
But
The air inside the house is hard and cold
And it used to be warm and soft
With her talking,
Saying nothing,
Asking silly questions –
'Is that you?' she'd ask,
And I'd say, 'No, it's Santa Claus,'
Or 'the man-in-the-moon,'
But I felt like me
Then.
A lot of the time now I don't.

ELISE MACLAY

Lament: Psalm 28

O God, hear me!
I am tormented by the finality of death
and harassed by those who want to explain it…
As though the pain of his death is not enough,
their glibness cuts like a razor into my heart
and the bleeding starts again.
O God, have pity on me
and keep them from my doorstep!

Why, O God, do I have to deal with them?
They crouch by my door;
their whispered voices fly in through my window:
'He was in the wrong place at the wrong time!'
O God of my life!
Tell me you were there, too!
Tell me that on your earth there is no wrong place
nor is there any wrong time
for the children of God!
Tell me you caught him in your arms
and wiped the tears from his eyes,
and showed him your face
as you had showed him your heart.
Tell me you are always with us
in life and in death.
Have pity on me, O God,
and keep them from my doorstep!
O God, they're like magpies,
suggesting his death is a test of my faith,
as though you are some egomaniac God
who zaps me from on high,
who demands repeated assurances of my love,
as though you do not know my heart!

Have pity on me, O God, and keep them from
  my doorstep!
O God, I know you are not what they say!
That you loved him so much that you wanted him
to live in heaven with you!
O God, they blaspheme you and trivialize his death!
I know you, O God of love,
I know you, and your will is life;
your name is compassion.
O God of mercy, send them away!
Let them leave me to my weeping.
Let them leave me with the quiet ones
who sit beside me through the days.
Let them leave me with your word open upon my heart.
Send them away,
but write once more upon their hearts
and upon mine the word of your love.

O merciful God,
there is no trouble I cannot bring to you!
In you only is my trust!

ANN WEEMS

What do I do now with my regrets? When the person
is dead, what do we do with our regrets?

… I believe that God forgives me. I do not doubt
that. The matter between God and me is closed. But…
my regrets remain. What do I do with my God-forgiven
regrets? Maybe some of what I regret doesn't even need
forgiving; maybe sometimes I did as well as I could. Full
love isn't always possible in this fallen world of ours.
Still, I regret.

I shall live with them. I shall accept my regrets as part
of my life, to be numbered among my self-inflicted wounds.

But I will not endlessly gaze at them. I shall allow the memories to prod me into doing better with those still living. And I shall allow them to sharpen the vision and intensify the hope for that Great Day coming when we can all throw ourselves into each other's arms and say, 'I'm sorry.'

The God of love will surely grant us such a day. Love needs that.

NICHOLAS WOLTERSTORFF

The tears… streamed down, and I let them flow as freely as they would, making of them a pillow for my heart. On them it rested.

ST AUGUSTINE OF HIPPO (354–430)

As the rain hides the stars, as the autumn mist hides the hills, as the clouds veil the blue of the sky, so the dark happenings of my lot hide the shining of your face from me. Yet, if I may hold your hand in the darkness, it is enough. Since I know that, though I may stumble in my going, you do not fall.

GAELIC PRAYER

I shall look at the world through tears. Perhaps I shall see things that dry-eyed I could not see.

NICHOLAS WOLTERSTORFF

Dear Lord, just as you gave us tear ducts to cry, you gave us ribs and stomachs to shake with laughter. My grief is serious work. I have a need for light and lightness in order to keep my balance. Whatever can help me laugh, even as I cry, I will be thankful for. Give me laughter and joy in my grief. In your name I pray. Amen.

PHILIP W. WILLIAMS

Her face thins almost
as we watch. Bones
seem larger – grating
on pillow and sheet

like shells on an edge
of shore. We speak

more simply in her presence:
a primer of nouns

and verbs. She lets go
of life gently. We

receive from her hands
the victory of belief,

learning the meaning of
our lives from our grief.

SISTER MAURA SSND

She whom we love and lose
is no longer where she was before.
She is now wherever we are.

ST JOHN CHRYSOSTOM (C. 347–407)

Today I read about a man who slashed his wrists
    because he lost his hat.
He was old, and of course, they say he was crazy.
I think not.
I think he'd just had all the losses he could take.
He said as much.
His last words were, 'O God, now I've lost my hat, too.'
I know how he felt.
Every time you turn around, time – with a little help
    from your friends – grabs off something else.

Something precious. At least to you.
Hearing. Sight. Beauty. Job. House. Even the corner
grocery turns into a parking lot and is lost.
Finally, you lose the thing you can't do without – hope
(that it can get better).
Dear God, when he gets to heaven, let that man find his
hat on the gatepost.

ELISE MACLAY

O God who brought us to birth,
and in whose arms we die:
in our grief and shock
contain and comfort us;
embrace us with your love,
give us hope in our confusion,
and grace to let go into new life,
through Jesus Christ. Amen.

JANET MORLEY

The Lord bless you and keep you. The Lord make his
face shine upon you and be gracious unto you, in your
going out and in your coming in, in your rising and in
your lying down, in your mourning and in your peace,
in your labour and in your leisure, in your laughter and
in your tears, until you too come to stand before him
in the day to which there is no sunset and no dawn. In
the name of the Father, and of the Son, and of the Holy
Ghost. Amen.

PHILIP W. WILLIAMS

New Beginnings

The healing power of forgiveness

May God bless us with forgiveness for our sins, reconciliation with those from whom we are divided, and solidarity with all who suffer. Amen.

MARCHIENE VROON RIENSTRA

Lord, grant that anger or other bitterness does not reign over us, but that by your grace, genuine kindness, loyalty and every kind of friendliness, generosity and gentleness may reign in us. Amen.

MARTIN LUTHER (1483–1546)

Holy Presence within me, I am willing to release all feelings of hurt and anger and resentment. Help me know true forgiveness and see each person as part of you. Let my words and my actions serve only to glorify you. May they heal and comfort and harmonize my life and the lives of those around me. Thank you, God.

AUTHOR UNKNOWN

He makes me so damned angry, Lord. Forgive me. I cannot explain it or justify it and I recognize it as a lack of love and therefore a sin. What am I to do? The minute I see him my nerves stand on edge and when we talk my temper tries at once to break loose from its tenuous moorings. Yet to avoid talking is unkind and cowardly. Give me forbearance I beg you, so that I do not judge or argue with everything he says, but try to understand what he is saying and how I might respond in love.

HELEN THOMAS

Thinking of someone you want to forgive, breathe a simple prayer:

Lord, help me see him/her as you do.

I cannot forgive this person. Please enable me to forgive.

_____, I bless you and release you to the Holy Spirit.

Lord, you have forgiven me. Help me to forgive myself.

Lord of creation,
remind all lovers of the power in their marriage.
Tell them of
   the joy, the romance, the fun
   of being man and wife;
   the new places to go,
   new things to do,
   new hopes, new laughter.
Give them
   new touches, new feelings,
   the new gifts, new surprises,
   and new beginnings.
Lord of redemption,
remind all lovers of redemption in marriage.
Tell them of
   the healing, understanding,
   the reconciling, the wiping of tears,
   the dying and rising,
   the fighting and forgiving,
   the kissing and making up,
   the repenting and absolving.
Give them
   the crucifying and the resurrecting,
   the hurting and the healing,

and the new chance.
Lord of creation and redemption,
have man and woman be Christ to one another. Amen.

HERBERT BROKERING

Our Father in heaven, you gave each of your earth
children the human power to forgive. We thank you that
we are humanly able to forgive each other our mean and
hateful acts. But we cannot forgive ourselves, Lord! We
cannot forgive our own meanness and hatefulness. We
cannot heal the cancer at the marrowbone of our beings.

But even that you have taken care of, Father of us all.
In your love for us you have freely forgiven us in your
son Jesus Christ, a miracle so amazing that we have not
grasped the wonder of it, a condition so brand new in
human history that we do not know how to receive it or
to use it.

Oh, teach us, dear Father! Teach us that you are not
only a God of forgiveness but that you in very fact and
act can accomplish it in us. We pray not for a Sunday
sense of forgiveness. We pray not for momentary acts
of forgiveness. We pray for the spirit of forgiveness. We
pray for the power of will to emigrate from our present
state and to move into the new state your son Jesus
Christ created for us, the state of forgiveness. We pray
that we may become fully naturalized citizens of the
state of forgiveness. We pray in your son's name. Amen.

EDNA HONG

The Jesus prayer

Lord Jesus Christ, Son of God,
have mercy on me, a sinner.

In this prayer, one of the great treasures of the Orthodox church, the words 'have mercy' (*eleison* in Greek) come from the same root as *elaion*, olive tree, and the oil from it. So they speak of healing, soothing, grace.

Each word or phrase in the prayer should be dwelt upon and its meaning allowed to penetrate through the mind to the heart which is the centre of being.

> Lord… Jesus… Christ… Son of God…
> heal, strengthen, forgive… me… a sinner
>
> repeated slowly, recollectedly, lovingly…
> silently, deeply, gratefully.
>
> GEORGE APPLETON (1902–93)

Today, O Lord, I accept your acceptance of me.
I confess that you are always with me and always for me.
I receive into my spirit your grace, your mercy, your care.
I rest in your love, O Lord. I rest in your love. Amen.

RICHARD J. FOSTER

Lord Jesus, we are silly sheep who have dared to stand before you and try to bribe you with our preposterous portfolios. Suddenly we have come to our senses. We are sorry and ask you to forgive us. Give us the grace to admit we are ragamuffins, to embrace our brokenness, to celebrate your mercy when we are at our weakest, to rely on your mercy no matter what we may do. Dear Jesus, gift us to stop grandstanding and trying to get attention, to do the truth quietly without display, to let the dishonesties in our lives fade away, to accept our limitations, to cling to the gospel of grace, and to delight in your love. Amen.

BRENNAN MANNING

The blessing of God,
whose love reconciles all who are divided,
be with you as you seek to heal
the brokenness around you.

VIENNA COBB ANDERSON

I Rest My Soul

Healing and stillness

Be silent.
Be still.
Alone,
Empty
Before your God
Say nothing.
Ask nothing.
Be silent.
Be still.
Let your God
Look upon you.
That is all.
God knows,
Understands,
Loves you with
An enormous love.
God only wants to
Look upon you
With Love.
Quiet.
Still.
Be.

Let your God –
Love you.

EDWINA GATELEY

My ego is like a fortress.
I have built its walls stone by stone
To hold out the invasion of the love of God.

But I have stayed here long enough.
There is light over the barriers. O my God –
The darkness of my house forgive

And overtake my soul.
I relax the barriers.
I abandon all that I think I am,
All that I hope to be,
All that I believe I possess.
I let go of the past,
I withdraw my grasping hand from the future,
And in the great silence of this moment,
I alertly rest my soul.

HOWARD THURMAN (1900–81)

O you who are at home
Deep in my heart
Enable me to join you
Deep in my heart.

THE TALMUD

God, teach me to let my soul rest, to still my
    worries and doubts,
to stop my constant clatter of questions and protests.
Let me come to you sometimes and just sit quietly,
like a mother smiling at her sleeping baby and
    listening to its soft breathing…
or like a small child intent on hearing a kitten's purr
    or a little bird's chirp…
or as if I were trying to hear a soft breeze moving
    across a pond,
a leaf dropping onto the grass.
Let me learn to wait patiently and trustingly for you
to make things clearer to me.
Teach me to be as calm as a lake after sundown…
as trusting as a baby in its mother's lap.
Teach me to grow gradually, unprotestingly, like
    a flower…

to go unresistingly wherever you send me,
like airborne seed obeying the breeze.
Teach me to turn always towards you,
the very essence of love and of life,
the cause of love and life,
the nourisher of love and life,
the purpose of love and life –
the way leaves keep turning towards the life-giving sun.

JOAN BEL GEDDES

I thank you that, by the inpouring of your love, you are
healing me of all that is contrary to your Spirit.

M.V. DUNLOP

Gentle me,
Holy One,
into an unclenched moment
a deep breath,
a letting go
of heavy experiences,
of dead certainties,
that, softened by the silence,
surrounded by the light,
and open to the mystery,
I may be found by wholeness,
upheld by the unfathomable,
entranced by the simple,
and filled with the joy
that is you.

TED LODER

Help me now to be quiet, relaxed and receptive, accepting the thought of healing grace at work, deep within my nature.

LESLIE WEATHERHEAD (1883–1975)

O Lord, Jesus Christ, who art as the shadow of a great rock in a weary land, who beholdest thy weak creatures weary of labour, weary of pleasure, weary of hope deferred, weary of self; in thine abundant compassion, and fellow feeling with us, and unutterable tenderness, bring us, we pray thee, unto thy rest. Amen.

CHRISTINA ROSSETTI (1830–94)

Drop thy still dews of quietness
    Till all our strivings cease;
Take from our souls the strain and stress,
And let our ordered lives confess
    The beauty of thy peace.

Breathe through the heats of our desire
    Thy coolness and thy balm;
Let sense be dumb, let flesh retire;
Speak through the earthquake, wind and fire,
    O still small voice of calm!

JOHN GREENLEAF WHITTIER (1807–92)

A way to become still

Say slowly and thoughtfully the first two verses of Psalm 63:

O God, you are my God:
early will I seek you.

My soul thirsts for you, my flesh longs for you:
in a dry and thirsty land where no water is.

Say it again. Then repeat a few of the key words:
O God, you are my God…
My soul longs for you…

Repeat these phrases several times, until you feel that
they are becoming part of you, sinking from your head
to your heart like water into a dry plant.
O God, you are my God…
My soul longs for you…

When you are ready, let the prayer become even shorter:
My God, or, simply, God.
Let yourself enter into the silence, using the name
of God to draw you again and again into the presence,
which is beyond words.
When distractions come (which they will), offer
them to God and then let go of them, returning to the
full verse or to the simpler words, so that they can lead
you back into silent communion with God. Many passages
from the Bible can be prayed over in this way.

ANGELA ASHWIN

Grant me the ability to be alone.
May it be my custom to go outdoors each day
among the trees and grasses,
among all growing things
and there may I be alone,
and enter into prayer
to talk with the one
that I belong to.

RABBI NACHMAN OF BRATZLAV (1772–1811)

Blessèd sister, holy mother, spirit of the fountain,
    spirit of the garden,
Suffer us not to mock ourselves with falsehood
Teach us to care and not to care
Teach us to sit still
Even among these rocks,
Our peace in his will
And even among these rocks
Sister, mother
And spirit of the river, spirit of the sea,
Suffer me not to be separated

And let my cry come unto thee.

T.S. ELIOT (1888–1965)

Breath prayers for stillness

Lord, come to me, my door is open.

Into your hands I commend my spirit.

Now the silence, now the peace.

Lord, I wait for your healing, your peace and your Word.

Let not your heart be troubled, neither let it be afraid.

Ah, dearest Jesus, holy child,
Make thee a bed, soft, undefiled,
Within my heart, that it may be
A quiet chamber kept for thee.

MARTIN LUTHER (1483–1546)

Those Who Watch

Prayers for the healing of others

Watch, O Lord, with those who wake,
　or watch, or weep tonight,
And give your angels and saints charge
　over those who sleep.
Tend your sick ones, O Lord Christ,
Rest your weary ones,
Bless your dying ones,
Soothe your suffering ones,
Pity your afflicted ones,
Shield your joyous ones,
And all for your love's sake.

ST AUGUSTINE OF HIPPO (354–430)

God of the desert, suffering God, bless this friend
　who hurts and longs for the day when she will be
　free of distress in mind and body.
God of healing and wholeness, fill her empty places
　with hope and embrace her with your comfort and
　courage.
Like the woman ill for twelve years who touched the
　hem of Jesus' garment, may she touch the garment
　of your compassion and feel spiritual power flow
　through her body and spirit.
We place our trust in you, God of tender love. Amen.

KATHLEEN FISCHER

O Mother and Father of all things, you whose joy
created the universe, thank you for blessing us with this
boy. We place him now in your loving arms. Guide the
surgeons' hands; let them find what they must to make
possible his healing. We ask nothing for ourselves. We
will do whatever is required of us, without complaint, in
gratitude for the happiness our children have brought us.

We ask only mercy for him. He has suffered so much, and he has so much to give. We beg you, let him live, that he may glorify your creation. Amen.

PHIL CATALFO

Thank you, Lord. I believe that your power is entering into this person, working towards the wholeness that I see in my mind. Amen.

AGNES SANFORD (1897–1982)

At a healing service, when laying on hands, I will often pray:

'May the healing love and grace of God be in every corner of your heart, crevice of your mind and cell of your body.'

AVERY BROOKE

Dear God,
friends with AIDS
slip through my fingers
faster than grains of sand,
and seemingly as many.

I can't hold them.

God, dear God,
please catch them
with your open hands,
within your welcoming embrace,
with your loving heart.

I wish I could be there for them.

I pray they'll be there for me
when I slip.
You too, my God,
our God. Amen.

CHRIS GLASER

I lift up my heart, O God, for all who are the prey of
anxious fears, who cannot get their minds off themselves
and for whom every demand made on them fills them
with foreboding, and with the feeling that they cannot
cope with all that is required of them.

Give them the comfort of knowing that this feeling
is illness, not cowardice; that millions have felt as they
feel, that there is a way through this dark valley, and light
at the end of it.

Lead them to those who can help them and understand
them and show them the pathway to health and happiness.
Comfort and sustain them by the loving presence of the
Saviour who knows and understands all our woe and fear,
and give them enough courage to face each day, and rest
their minds in the thought that you will see them through.

LESLIE WEATHERHEAD (1883–1975)

We remember those who are deep in depression,
  whose inner world is bleak and dark… especially…
We remember those who have recently said farewell
  to a loved one and who feel that joy will never
  return… especially…
We remember those who are caught up in running
  through life and are entangled in frenzied activity…
We remember those who struggle to believe in their
  own goodness…
We remember those who have lost their dreams and their
  enthusiasm for life…

We remember those who are experiencing failure in
   relationships or in work situations…
We remember those who doubt their inner growth
   and who question their journey with God…
We remember those who never seem to get beyond
   financial worries and the pain of caring for the
   essentials of life…
We remember those who have been rejected, deserted,
   betrayed or abandoned…
We remember those who live in the grips of addiction
   and the throes of self-absorption…
We remember those who have lost hope and who daily
   do battle with thoughts of suicide…
We remember those who live constantly with worry
   and anxiety.

JOYCE RUPP

Hear my voice, O God, when I groan because I feel
   so helpless.
Why should one you created suffer so deeply
the disorientation and lostness of a mind confused?
We who know how to make bombs well enough
to blast our planet into oblivion,
why do you not give us the ability
to prevent degenerative disease?
Fragmented, brittle hours of lostness enshroud her day.
Seventy-eight, a flickering candle burning at twilight.
Yet, I remember, there were the good days.
Lark singing overhead
and wild spring flowers in the hedge.
'A pearl,' she said, 'this day is a pearl,
strung on my necklace of translucent memories.'
When she saw mountains for the first time,
'I can't believe it,' she cried,

face radiant with gratitude.
We hiked summers away through mist and rain
and walked in winter snow.

It's hard to reach her now as she struggles
in the dark, seeping swamps of confusion.
Like timeless Job I hurl into emptiness
the unanswerable 'WHY?'
and in the waiting I remember —
there were the good days.

ELIZABETH J. CANHAM

We pray/accept responsibility for children
who sneak Popsicles before supper,
who erase holes in maths workbooks,
who can never find their shoes.
And we pray/accept responsibility for those
who stare at photographers from behind barbed wire,
who can't bound down the street in a new pair
of sneakers,
who never 'counted potatoes',
who were born in places we wouldn't be caught dead,
who never go to the circus,
who live in an X-rated world.
We pray/accept responsibility for children
who bring us sticky kisses and fistfuls of dandelions,
who hug us in a hurry and forget their lunch money.
And we pray/accept responsibility for those
who never get dessert,
who have no safe blanket to drag behind them,
who watch their parents watch them die,
who can't find any bread to steal,
who don't have any rooms to clean up,
whose pictures aren't on anybody's dresser,
and whose monsters are real.

We pray/accept responsibility for children
    who spend all their allowance before Tuesday,
    who throw tantrums in the grocery store and pick
      at their food,
    who like ghost stories,
    who shove dirty clothes under the bed
    and never rinse out the tub,
    who get visits from the tooth fairy,
    who don't like to be kissed in front of the car pool,
    who squirm in church or temple and scream in
      the phone,
    whose tears we sometimes laugh at and whose
      smiles can make us cry.
And we pray/accept responsibility for those
    whose nightmares come in the daytime,
    who will eat anything,
    who have never seen a dentist,
    who aren't spoiled by anybody,
    who go to bed hungry and cry themselves to sleep,
    who live and move, but have no being.
We pray/accept responsibility for children
    who want to be carried and for those who must,
    for those we never give up on and for those
    who don't get a second chance,
    for those we smother and for those who will grab
      the hand of anyone kind enough to offer it.

ADAPTED FROM INA J. HUGHES

Lord,
make more families.
Make them close
that there can be healing and helping
and loving and resting and singing
and eating and drinking

in your name.
In families
prepare the people for the world.

Send them well loved
into a world in need of much love.
Where there is no father or no mother,
make it a family.
Where there is no family room,
no family album, no uncles and aunts,
let there be a family.
Where there are no birthdays and holidays
and family mealtimes,
bring together enough to make a family.
Make families by love.
May we all belong
somewhere, somehow, to someone.
O Christ, be here in this place
and make it a home. Amen.

HERBERT BROKERING

May those who doubt
    Trust in their doubt.
May those who cannot believe
    Trust in their disbelief.
May those who are tempted
    Trust their temptation.
May those who are alone
    Trust their aloneness.
May those who are abandoned
    Trust their abandonment.
May those who are desolate
    Trust their desolation.
For by this prayer alone

All darkness is presented to you, O God.
And as you lead the lost so may you lead them
  By means of that which they do not possess
  To that which they despair ever to find.
May your truth enlighten all paths
  And bring courage in all fears.

Daniel J. McGill

I saw you in the doorway.
You were black and bruised and broken.
I knew you were someone's daughter.

You are your mother's daughter.
If she could, she would sit with you
and say how much she loved you.

I saw you in the shelter.
You looked much older than your years.
Your kids were tired and making a fuss.
I knew you were someone's daughter.

You are your mother's daughter.
Imagine her here, as a sister and friend,
saying how much she loves you.

I saw you on the news last night
on a dirt road in Soweto.
They were screaming at you.
You had no shoes.
I knew you were someone's daughter.

You are your mother's daughter
and she is her mother's daughter.
She has put up with so much abuse.
That shows how much she loves you.

I saw you in the delivery room
in drug withdrawal, writhing.
They say you have AIDS. You are three hours old,
and I know you are someone's daughter.

You are your mother's daughter
and she needs you to forgive her.
She doesn't know how to love as yet,
but when she does, I promise you,
she will say how much she loves you.

I saw you in an orphanage.
How sad you looked, and lonely.
They say that you are hard to place,
but I know you are someone's daughter.

You are your mother's daughter
and a foster mother's daughter,
and one of these days, she will come for you
and say how much she loves you.

I saw you in a nursing home.
You were slumped in a chair with a vacant stare.
I knew you were somebody's daughter.

You are your mother's daughter,
your Mother God's own daughter.
Soon, very soon, she will come for you
and say how much she loves you.

MIRIAM THERESE WINTER

Lord Jesus Christ, thou Son of the Most High, Prince
of Peace, be born again into our world. Wherever there is
war in this world, wherever there is pain, wherever there
is loneliness, wherever there is no hope, come, thou long-
expected one, with healing in thy wings.

Holy Child, whom the shepherds and the kings and the dumb beasts adored, be born again. Wherever there is boredom, wherever there is fear of failure, wherever there is temptation too strong to resist, wherever there is bitterness of heart, come, thou blessed one, with healing in thy wings.

Saviour, be born in each of us who raises his face to thy face, not knowing fully who he is or who thou art, knowing only that thy love is beyond his knowing and that no other has the power to make him whole. Come, Lord Jesus, to each who longs for thee even though he has forgotten thy name. Come quickly. Amen.

FREDERICK BUECHNER

O Lord, this world is full of fear.
Make my fear into a prayer for the fearful.

HENRI NOUWEN (1932–96)

Intercession

Holding a name lovingly, trustingly before God,
without diagnosing the person's need,

or telling God what to do,

leaving God to do what in love is
most needed.

The name may be repeated many times,
on the lips or in the mind,
and then, held silently in the heart.

If our Lord's name is added after the name of the
one for whom we are praying,
his love is invoked to magnify our own human love.

GEORGE APPLETON (1902–93)

O suffering Christ, lay your hand in healing power upon those who feel they can bear no more, until their hearts are hushed and quieted, knowing that round about them and underneath them are the Everlasting Arms. Amen.

LESLIE WEATHERHEAD (1883–1975)

Lord, I bring before you
the needs of my parents, friends,
brothers, sisters,
all whom I love,
and all who have asked me to pray for them.
I pray that they may experience your help
and the gift of your comfort,
protection from all dangers,
deliverance from all sin,
and freedom from pain.
May they give you joyful thanks and praise.
I also bring before you
all those who have in any way
offended or insulted me,
or done me any harm.
I also remember those
whom I have hurt or offended or troubled
by what I said or did
knowingly or unknowingly.
Lord, in your mercy, forgive all our sins against
    one another.
Take from our hearts
all suspicion, hard feelings,
anger, dissension,
and whatever else may diminish the love
we should have for one another.
Have mercy, O Lord, on all who ask your mercy.

Give grace to all who need it,
that we may finally come to eternal life.

THOMAS À KEMPIS (1380–1471)

Breath prayers for intercession

_____: May the power of God protect you.
May the love of Jesus heal you.
May the wisdom of the spirit guide you.
Now and for ever.

Lord Jesus Christ, have mercy on [him, her, them].

Not my will but yours be done.

Jesus, Healer, make _____ whole.

May _____ be safe from inner and outer enemies.
May _____ be strong and healthy in body.
May _____ be peaceful and calm in mind.
May _____ take care of himself/herself with happy ease.
May _____ come to union with God.

May peace prevail on earth.

Dear Lord,
Help me to release my need to control.
Help me to let go and to accept your will.
I now place this situation lovingly into your hands.
I pray for the highest and the best for all concerned.
Thank you. Amen.

ROBERT AND JANET ELLSWORTH

Life, spilling over the hills of our grief
and filling the wells
in our souls and our senses,

come, lift us up into light-hearted laughter,
so all the weight of our awareness
does not overwhelm us.
Life of Our World, be life
in and through us,
now and for ever. Amen.

MIRIAM THERESE WINTER

May you face life without illusion,
    but with gratitude.
Though you have known tragedy,
    may you nonetheless cherish laughter.
May you have an ever clearer sense of what
    is important and what is not.
May your encounters with evil
    heighten your appreciation of what is good.
May you learn to meet death in a way that
    leads you to celebrate life.

KATHLEEN FISCHER

In the nursing home

She is like a horse grazing
a hill pasture that someone makes
smaller by coming every night
to pull the fences in and in.

She has stopped running wide loops,
stopped even the tight circles.
She drops her head to feed; grass
is dust, and the creekbed's dry.

Master, come with your light
halter. Come and bring her in.

JANE KENYON (1947–95)

Oh Lord who took on human flesh in the person of our Saviour Jesus Christ so that you could walk the last mile to death with each of us, assist your servant who is now on that last mile. Give her courage and faith and especially hope that she may face death bravely and teach the rest of us how to die. Bring her home to you where her life will only just begin, and bring her home as gently as possible. We ask this in the name of Jesus the Lord. Amen.

ANDREW M. GREELEY

Dear Lord, welcome this traveller who has roamed the whole world with an eager and observant eye and a responsive heart. Welcome him as he goes forth now on a new journey to an unknown place.

It is always so hard to say goodbye to someone we love, but we are willing to do so if we know he is embarking on the next stage of a fascinating journey and that he is always curious to see things he has never seen before, happy to voyage to places where he has never been before, ready to love appreciatively what he has never known before, and to rejoice in what he loves. So help me to accept the fact that he is parting from me now, travelling far away from me, and help me to hope that we will be rejoined some day.

His journey in recent months has been hard, and he is tired. Comfort him now. And also comfort me, who will miss him so very much, and help me to remember, and to share, and to keep alive his spirit of adventure and love of life. Amen!

JOAN BEL GEDDES

Receive into Paradise, O Lord,
all those who will sleep tonight
and not awaken again.

Eternal rest give to them, O Lord;
and let perpetual light shine upon them.

TRADITIONAL PRAYER

Your Grace Has No End

Gratitude for healings and blessings

O Lord, Creator,
Ruler of the world, Father,
I thank, thank, thank you
that you have brought me through.
How strong the pain was –
but you were stronger.
How deep the fall was –
but you were even deeper.
How dark was the night –
but you were the noonday sun in it.
You are our father, our mother,
our brother, and our friend.
Your grace has no end,
and your light no snuffer.
We praise you, we honour you,
and we pray to your holy name.
We thank you that you rule thus,
and that you are so merciful
with your tired followers.

GHANAIAN PRAYER

May he be blessed for ever who has taken such
care of me.
May he be blessed for ever who has put up with
so much from me!

ST TERESA OF AVILA (1515–82)

I suffered, and now there is joy,
I was lonely, and now there is comfort,
I was desolate, and now there is warmth,
I was empty, and now there is fullness.

The years and months of pain dragged on
And plunged me into dark solitude,
And now, why now, do I see the light and feel
    the warmth?
Is it that my despair reached its depth
And God, in pity, said: Enough?
Where was my soul then
When my spirit was so dead?
And now there is a relief,
An almost tangible gratitude that it is over
And that a spark of life and love
Is being born from nothing.

This will not last for ever.
But thank you, God, for living again,
For letting me know and feel
Your life and presence in me.
And if this hope should die again,
Let me remember the years of emptiness that passed.
Stay now, God, a little longer.

EDWINA GATELEY

For all the good things I do have and
for all the good things I have had and
for all the good things I will have,
for what I am,
for what I have been,
for what I can be,
for what I shall be,
    thank you, God.

JOAN BEL GEDDES

O God, early in the morning I cry to you.
Help me to pray
And to concentrate my thoughts on you;
I cannot do this alone.
In me there is darkness,
But with you there is light;
I am lonely, but you do not leave me;
I am feeble in heart, but with you there is help;
I am restless, but with you there is peace.
In me there is bitterness, but with you there is patience;
I do not understand your ways,
But you know the way for me.

O heavenly Father,
I praise and thank you
For the peace of the night;
I praise and thank you for this new day;
I praise and thank you for all your goodness
and faithfulness throughout my life.

You have granted me many blessings;
Now let me also accept what is hard
from your hand...
You make all things work together for good
for your children.

DIETRICH BONHOEFFER (1906–45)

The following prayers are intended only as the beginning
of a pattern of prayer. You will be able to create your own
in a short time. If you pray in this way, you will find your
life filled to overflowing with gifts and wonders. Brief
blessing prayers are a part of the heritage of every disciple
of Jesus, for they were a part of his daily prayer life.

I lift up my heart to you in gratitude
   for this gift of a new day filled with possibilities.
I lift up my heart to you in gratitude, O God,
   for this gift of a hot shower that refreshes me.
I lift up my heart to you in gratitude
   for the gift of this glass of wine
   and its taste of sun, grape and earth.
I lift up my heart to you in gratitude
   for the gift of music
   that delights my ear, my heart and my soul.
I lift up my heart to you in gratitude
   for the ability to read
   and for the wonder of words that speak to my heart.
I lift up my heart to you in gratitude
   for the expression of love I have just shared.
I lift up my heart to you in gratitude
   for the present pain I feel,
   which frames with greater joy the pleasures of my life.

EDWARD HAYS

Today is an ordinary day. I thank you, God,
for the ordinary.
I thank you for a day of plain sunlight,
of simple tasks and easy mindless chores.
Sabbath God, I thank you for a day of rest.
No nightmares today.
No new growth today.
No terror today.
I thank you for this ordinary day. Amen.

CATHERINE J. FOOTE

In the godforsaken, obscene quicksand of life,
there is a deafening alleluia
rising from the souls
of those who weep,
and of those who weep with those who weep.
If you watch, you will see
the hand of God
putting the stars back in their skies
one by one.

ANN WEEMS

As my mind and heart roam around my life,
I think about, see, hear, feel,
the people who inhabited it –

I think of them gently, now,
how each one blessed me… in one way or another.
By who and how they were… and are.

Now I bless them
in one way or another
and ask you, my God,
to bless us all.

MARLENE HALPIN

It is written that 'Everywhere, hands lie open to catch
us when we fall'. Let us give thanks tonight for this
invisible support.

M.J. RYAN

We give thanks for our friends.
Our dear friends.
We anger each other.
We fail each other.

We share this sad earth, this tender life,
    this precious time.
Such richness. Such wildness.
Together we are blown about.
Together we are dragged along.
All this delight.
All this suffering.
All this forgiving life.
We hold it together. Amen.

MICHAEL LEUNIG

To be joyful in the universe is a brave and reckless act. The courage for joy springs not from the certainty of human experience, but the surprise. Our astonishment at being loved, our bold willingness to love in return — these wonders promise the possibility of joyfulness, no matter how often and how harshly love seems to be lost.

Therefore, despite the world's sorrows, we give thanks for our loves, for our joys and for the continued courage to be happily surprised.

MOLLY FUMIA

And in the evening, when I lie in bed and end my prayers with the words, 'I thank you, God, for all that is good and dear and beautiful,' I am filled with joy. Then I think about 'the good' of going into hiding, of my health and with my whole being of the 'dearness' of Peter, of that which is still embryonic and impressionable and which we neither of us dare to name or touch, of that which will come sometime; love, the future, happiness and of 'the beauty' which exists in the world; the world, nature, beauty and all, all that is exquisite and fine.

I don't think then of all the misery, but of the beauty that still remains. This is one of the things that Mummy and I are so entirely different about. Her counsel when one feels melancholy is: 'Think of all the misery in the world and be thankful that you are not sharing in it!'

My advice is: 'Go outside, to the fields, enjoy nature and the sunshine, go out and try to recapture happiness in yourself and in God. Think of all the beauty that's still left in and around you and be happy!'

I don't see how Mummy's idea can be right, because then how are you supposed to behave if you go through the misery yourself? Then you are lost. On the contrary, I've found that there is always some beauty left – in nature, sunshine, freedom, in yourself; these can all help you. Look at these things, then you find yourself again, and God, and then you regain your balance.

And whoever is happy will make others happy too. He who has courage and faith will never perish in misery!

ANNE FRANK (1929–C. 1945)

Lord, I am grateful to you
that in your mysterious love
you have taken away from me
all earthly wealth,
and that you now clothe and feed me
through the kindness of others.

Lord, I am grateful to you
that since you have taken away from me
the sight of my eyes,
you care for me now
through the eyes of others.

Lord, I am grateful to you
that since you have taken away from me
the strength of my hands and heart,
you care for me now
through the hands and hearts of others.

Lord, I pray for them,
that you will reward them in your love,
that they may continue to faithfully serve and care
until they come to a happy end
in eternity with you.

MECHTHILD OF MAGDEBURG (1210–80)

Send Me Someone

The healing power of compassion

Hurting, they came to him,
Healed, they followed him.
Grateful, they gave to him what they had and
   what they were.
Blessed, they became a blessing
and went out to all the world in his name.

Those who are hurt
and healed
grateful
and blessed
still move among us
in his name.

ANN WEEMS

Out of the ashes rises the healer.

FLORA SLOSSON WUELLNER

Lord,
when I am famished,
   give me someone who needs food;
when I am thirsty,
   send me someone who needs water;
when I am cold,
   send me someone to warm;
when I am hurting,
   send me someone to console;
when my cross becomes heavy,
   give me another's cross to share;
when I am poor,
   lead someone needy to me;
when I have no time,
   give me someone to help for a moment;
when I am humiliated,

give me someone to praise;
when I am discouraged,
   send me someone to encourage;
when I need another's understanding,
   give me someone who needs mine;
when I need somebody to take care of me,
   send me someone to care for;
when I think of myself,
   turn my thoughts towards another.

JAPANESE PRAYER

Having eaten my last crumb
I hear a voice in the wilderness of my heart.
   Bring me a little water
   the voice pleads.
I am off for the water
when again I am interrupted.
   Bring me a scrap of bread
   the voice calls.
I freeze inside, barely able to believe
   the demands of God.
It is kindness to give someone a drink, yes
But to give out of an empty house is agony.

Someone is asking for a crust of bread
And I have only a few tears
   a handful of flour
   a little oil.
The sticks in my hand are to build a fire,
   to bake a few crumbs for myself
   before I die.

But the call waits in my soul
   like a volcano.
I bake the bread in silence

with my tears
with my handful of flour
with my little oil.

The salt from my tears is the seasoning.
The hungry one eats and is nourished.

Suddenly I am hungry no longer
My vessel of flour is undiminishing
My jar of oil never runs dry.

When you have gathered up the crumbs
   of all you have and are
And baked your bread
   in the only place left:
   the oven of your heart,
Then you will know what it means
   to be bread for the world.
There is a wealth in poverty
   that ought not to be wasted.
There is a nourishment in crumbs
   that ought to be tasted.

MACRINA WIEDERKEHR

Mother Wisdom speaks:

Some of you I will hollow out.
I will make you a cave.
I will carve you so deep the stars will shine in
   your darkness.
You will be a bowl.
You will be the cup in the rock collecting rain.

I will hollow you with knives.
I will not do this to make you clean.
I will not do this to make you pure.

You are clean already.
You are pure already.

I will do this because the world needs the hollowness
   of you.
I will do this for the space that you will be.
I will do this because you must be large.
A passage.
People will find their way through you.
A bowl.
People will eat from you
and their hunger will not weaken them unto death.
A cup to catch the sacred rain.

My daughter, do not cry. Do not be afraid.
Nothing you need will be lost.
I am shaping you.
I am making you ready.

Light will flow in your hollowing.
You will be filled with light.
Your bones will shine.
The round, open centre of you will be radiant.
I will call you Brilliant One.
I will call you Daughter Who Is Wide.
I will call you Transformed.

CHRISTINE LORE WEBBER

Jesus, you cared for all the sick who came to you. I want
to care with loving compassion, to attend to details with
gentleness. But I become weary and impatient, angry and
abrupt. It is hard to watch the suffering of someone I love,
hard to find energy for all I must do. I grow discouraged
and resentful. Let me learn from your life of compassion.

Spirit of healing and comfort, be with me in these
difficult times. Teach me to take time for myself, to be
gentle with my own limits, to ask for help from others.

May your grace allow me to forgive myself when I fail,
to let go of my expectations, to grieve all my losses.
Send your healing power to me and the one for whom
I care. We trust in your love.

KATHLEEN FISCHER

May the pain of our loss
  Increase the fire of our love
May the pain of our guilt
  Ignite the flame of mercy in us
May the pain of our mistakes
  Light for us the path to wisdom
May the pain of our hatreds
  Awaken us to compassion
May the pain of our limitations
  Enkindle in us understanding
May the pain of our regrets
  Shine forth in forgiveness.

DANIEL J. MCGILL

Unbidden came God's love,
not rushing from the skies
as angel, flame or dove
but shining through your eyes.

THOMAS H. TROEGER

God, help us to enter into the troubles of others,
know them as if they were our own, and act accordingly.

AVERY BROOKE

Give me, Lord, a stout heart to bear my own burdens, a tender heart to bear the burdens of others and a believing heart to lay all my burdens on you, for you care for us.

LESSLIE NEWBIGIN

Pray for one another, so that you may be healed.

JAMES 5:16

You may call God love.
You may call God goodness.
But the best name for God is compassion.

MEISTER ECKHART (C. 1260–C. 1328)

Into Your Hands

Facing death

Into your hands, O God,
This solitude,
Into your hands, O God,
This emptiness.
Into your hands, O God,
This loneliness,
Into your hands –
This all.
Into your hands, O God,
This grief,
Into your hands
This sleeping fear.

Into your hands, O God –
What is left,
What is left
Of me.

EDWINA GATELEY

I have always known
that at last I would
take this road,
but yesterday
I did not know
it would be today.

JAPANESE PRAYER

Always, before this, I've just been sick for a while, a few
days or a week or so. Once it was a matter of months. But
now I realize that I may not get well. I may have to live
with this pain until I die and come to you.

I don't want to face that, God. Neither pain that doesn't
go away, nor death. I know that they come to us all, but
I am not ready – not anywhere near ready.

Help me, God. Give me the hope, the patience and the courage that I need. Help me not to be too envious of those who are well. Take away my anger and resentment so that I don't hurt those around me. Help me to use my reduced energies and opportunities to the best of my ability. And above all, give me greater love and understanding for my family, my friends, and all those I see from day to day.

AVERY BROOKE

Let us live in such a way
That when we die
Our love will survive
And continue to grow. Amen.

MICHAEL LEUNIG

The word of death
curves around my heart
like a question mark
whispers
who are you really
what do you care about
what do you really want
what matters
The word of death
presses its way quietly,
insistently into my mind
reminding me
there's no time to waste
in choosing love
this day is precious,
this moment — *this* one —
is all we have
why wait
why leave unspoken now

a single word
that love would speak
why leave undone
a single gesture
love would express
what could possibly matter more
than love now
than peace now
than forgiveness and freedom now
what foolish reasons
or excuses of fear
do not pale next to the truth
that love is here
that now is all there is eternally
How can I choose less
than to love
with all of my heart, mind and soul
you
and life
and everything
now

The word of death
comes into my life
bearing a sacred promise
and gift –
calls me to awaken today to life
and the truth of love
as all that matters
and is
and lives.

DIANE BERKE

O Lord God,
great distress has come upon me;
my cares threaten to crush me,
and I do not know what to do.
O God, be gracious to me and help me.
Give me strength to bear what you send,
and do not let fear rule over me;
take a father's care of my wife and children.

O merciful God,
forgive me all the sins that I have committed
against you and against my fellow men.
I trust in your grace
and commit my life wholly into your hands.
Do with me according to your will
and as is best for me.
Whether I live or die, I am with you,
and you, my God, are with me.
Lord, I wait for your salvation
and for your kingdom. Amen.

DIETRICH BONHOEFFER (1906–45)

Father, my Father! All things are possible for you.
Take this cup of suffering away from me.
Yet not what I want, but what you want.

MARK 14:36

I worry and I wish.
I wish I had taken care of more things
    before I got this sick.
I worry what will happen to them
    if I don't recover.

I think maybe tomorrow
I'll have the strength
to do something about it.

I know probably I won't.

Help me to be at peace
with all the things
that are left undone,
my God.

MARLENE HALPIN

Lord, I am ill and I don't know what is wrong with me
and no one will tell me. Help me, for I am afraid of
dying; afraid that I will cease to be and that the world
will go on as if I had never been. After the fullness and
joyfulness of living, this is a terrifying thought. Lord,
I am no longer sure that I believe you exist, or, if you
do, that you love and care for me; yet I think I have
experienced your love, come to know you in prayer.
But here I am back with my childhood fear of ending
in nothing. Please give me a firmer belief and a deeper
knowledge of you so that I may trust that when I die
I will come to live more fully with you than I have ever
done here.

MICHAEL HOLLINGS AND ETTA GULLICK

Lord,
If I have to die
Let me die;
But please,
Take away this fear.

KEN WALSH

Pain isolates,
No matter how many friends you have
Or how devoted.
Well-meaning, they sit beside your bed,
And press your hands,
You slip away,
Though your fingers stay entwined.
I have gone into the pain, deep and far,
How cold, how desolate it is here,
Starting at every sound,
Half hoping, half in fear,
Death, is that you?
Now, are you here?

ELISE MACLAY

My boat is very small,
Heavily laden with stones:
The waves run high around,
The stream is wide, and very swift:
Take thou the helm, my God,
Oh let thy mercy steer her on,
And bring her to the farther shore in peace.

GIRIDHAR, INDIA (17TH CENTURY)

O Lord, I've turned my eyes and my prayers to you so
very often. There have been times when I've felt forgotten
by you and I really wondered if you were still there to
hear me. Times when I got so discouraged I prayed to
die. Times when I was so broken and depressed I didn't
feel like talking to anyone. Times when I was so angry
I felt like screaming and crying at the same time. Times
when I felt so helpless, so hopeless I didn't even want
to try again. I have hoped so many times, bargained and
prayed in so many ways.

O Lord, as you hear my cry and see my tears, I pray that you may give me that peace of mind which comes from leaving things up to you. Help me to live one day at a time, to find new strength in you as my body weakens, to be grateful for all that is done to take away the pain and make me comfortable. Stay by my side as I walk through the dark valley so that your light may lead me to your undiscovered mountain. I ask this in Jesus' name. Amen.

FATHER ARNALDO PANGRAZZI

How to make these last days count, God? To live them with courage, and without complaint. To give and receive small joys. To teach the best already learned and to learn a little more.

AVERY BROOKE

Let evening come

Let the light of late afternoon
shine through chinks in the barn, moving
up the bales as the sun moves down.

Let the cricket take up chafing
as a woman takes up her needles
and her yarn. Let evening come.

Let dew collect on the hoe abandoned
in long grass. Let the stars appear
and the moon disclose her silver horn.

Let the fox go back to its sandy den.
Let the wind die down. Let the shed
go black inside. Let evening come.

To the bottle in the ditch, to the scoop
in the oats, to air in the lung
let evening come.

Let it come, as it will, and don't
be afraid. God does not leave us
comfortless, so let evening come.

JANE KENYON (1947–95)

Remain with us, Lord,
for evening approaches
and daylight dwindles.
Remain with us
and with your entire Church.
Remain with us
as daylight dwindles,
as our lives dwindle,
at the end of the world.

Remain with us,
through your grace and kindness,
through your sacred Word and sacrament,
through your help and benediction.

Remain with us
when we are visited
by night-time's torment and anguish,
night-time's doubts and temptations,
the painful night-time of death.

Remain with us and all the faithful
world without end. Amen.

WILHELM LÖHE (1808–72)

Abide with me; fast falls the eventide;
The darkness deepens; Lord, with me abide:
When other helpers fail, and comforts flee;
Help of the helpless, O abide with me.

Swift to its close ebbs out life's little day;
Earth's joys grow dim, its glories pass away;
Change and decay in all around I see;
O thou who changest not, abide with me.

I need thy presence every passing hour;
What but thy grace can foil the tempter's power?
Who like thyself my guide and stay can be?
Through cloud and sunshine, O abide with me.

I fear no foe, with thee at hand to bless;
Ills have no weight, and tears no bitterness:
Where is death's sting? Where, grave, thy victory?
I triumph still, if thou abide with me.

Hold thou thy cross before my closing eyes;
Shine through the gloom and point me to the skies;
Heaven's morning breaks, and earth's vain shadows flee;
In life, in death, O Lord, abide with me.

HENRY FRANCIS LYTE (1793–1847)

O Lord, support us all the day long of this troublous
life, until the shadows lengthen and the evening comes,
and the busy world is hushed, and the fever of life is
over, and our work is done. Then in thy mercy grant us
a safe lodging, and a holy rest, and peace at the last.
Through Jesus Christ our Lord. Amen.

JOHN HENRY NEWMAN (1801–90)

As thou wast before
At my life's beginning,
Be thou so again
   At my journey's end.

As thou wast besides
At my soul's shaping,
Father, be thou too
   At my journey's close.

Be with me a-watching
Each evening and morning,
And allure me home
   To the land of the saints.

Carmina Gadelica

O God, you who in your love have kept me vigorously
and joyfully at work in days gone by, and now send me
joyful and contented into silence and inactivity, grant
that I may find happiness in you in all my solitary and
quiet hours. In your strength, O God, I bid farewell to
all. The past you know: I leave it at your feet. Grant me
grace to respond to your divine call, to leave all that is
dear on earth, and to go out alone to you. Behold, I come
quickly, says the Lord. Come, Lord Jesus.

INDIAN PRIEST

Wild Nights – Wild Nights!
Were I with thee
Wild Nights should be
Our luxury!

Futile – the Winds –
To a Heart in port –

Done with the Compass –
Done with the Chart!

Rowing in Eden –
Ah, the Sea!
Might I but moor – Tonight –
In thee!

EMILY DICKINSON (1830–86)

Precious Lord, take my hand,
Lead me on, let me stand.
I am tired, I am weak, I am worn.

Through the storm, through the night,
Lead me on to the light.
Take my hand, Precious Lord, lead me home.

When my way grows drear, Precious Lord, linger near
When my life is almost gone.
Hear my cry, hear my call, hold my hand, lest I fall.
Take my hand, Precious Lord, lead me home.

When the darkness appears and the night draws near
And the day is past and gone,
At the river I stand,
Guide my feet, hold my hand.
Take my hand, Precious Lord, lead me home.

THOMAS A. DORSEY (1899–1993)

O Comforter of priceless worth
Send peace and unity on earth;
Support us in our final strife
And lead us out of death to life.

MARTIN LUTHER (1483–1546)

Today is a very good day to die.
Every living thing is in harmony with me.
Every voice sings a chorus within me.
All beauty has come to rest in my eyes.
All bad thoughts have departed from me.
Today is a very good day to die.
My land is peaceful around me.
My fields have been turned for the last time.
My house is filled with laughter.
My children have come home.
Yes, today is a very good day to die.

NANCY WOOD

Think of –
Stepping on shore, and finding it Heaven!
Of taking hold of a hand, and finding it God's hand,
Of breathing new air, and finding it celestial air,
Of feeling invigorated, and finding it immortality,
Of passing from storm and tempest to an unbroken calm,
Of waking up, and finding it Home.

AUTHOR UNKNOWN

Be each saint in heaven,
Each sainted woman in heaven,
Each angel in heaven
Stretching their arms for you,
Smoothing the way for you,
When you go thither
    Over the river hard to see;
Oh when you go thither home
    Over the river hard to see.

CARMINA GADELICA

O Lord, you have made us very small, and we bring our years to an end, like a tale that is told. Help us to remember that beyond our brief day is the eternity of your love.

REINHOLD NIEBUHR (1892–1971)

May my homeland continue to live beyond my life.
 Amen.
May children continue to live in my homeland many generations.
 Amen.
May it be blessed with abundance and health in its air, its water and its soil.
 Amen.
May the wild creatures it has borne bear many descendants and may they not be driven from their homes.
 Amen.
May the plants it gives life to, no matter how humble, prosper a thousand generations.
 Amen.
May every creature there dwelling, especially humans, love my homeland, for she is our mother.
 Amen.

DANIEL J. MCGILL

Long before we were born or our mothers and fathers were born or their mothers and fathers were born, you were.
 Before there were any people or any world you were here.
 And you made us with love and watched us and picked us up when we fell and helped us try again. And all our lives you will love us and when we leave the world we will come home to you. And our children and our children's children will love you, and come home to you. And your

kingdom will always wait for us and for all the people who ever were or ever will be.

AVERY BROOKE

All shall be Amen and Alleluia.
We shall rest and we shall see,
We shall see and we shall know.
We shall know and we shall love.
We shall love and we shall praise.
Behold our end which is no end.

ST AUGUSTINE OF HIPPO (354–430)

O God, our help in ages past,
  Our hope for years to come,
Our shelter from the stormy blast,
  And our eternal home.

Under the shadow of thy throne
  Thy saints have dwelt secure;
Sufficient is thine arm alone,
  And our defence is sure.

Before the hills in order stood,
  Or earth receiv'd her frame,
From everlasting thou art God,
  To endless years the same.

A thousand ages in thy sight
  Are like an evening gone;
Short as the watch that ends the night
  Before the rising sun.

Our God, our help in ages past,
  Our hope for years to come,
Be thou our guard while troubles last,
  And our eternal home.

ISAAC WATTS (1674–1748)

I am Resurrection and I am Life, says the Lord.
Whoever has faith in me shall have life,
even though he die.
And everyone who has life,
and has committed himself to me in faith,
shall not die for ever.

As for me, I know that my Redeemer lives
and that at the last he will stand upon the earth.
After my awaking, he will raise me up;
and in my body I shall see God.
I myself shall see, and my eyes behold him
who is my friend and not a stranger.

For none of us has life in himself,
and none becomes his own master when he dies.
For if we have life, we are alive in the Lord,
and if we die, we die in the Lord.
So, then, whether we live or die,
we are the Lord's possession.

Happy from now on
are those who die in the Lord!
So it is, says the Spirit,
for they rest from their labours.

THE BOOK OF COMMON PRAYER

Acknowledgments

Page 10: 'Almighty God, you are the source', from *Healing in the Landscape of Prayer*.
Copyright © 1996 Avery Brooke. Used by permission of Cowley Publications.
Page 10: 'Merciful God, Loving Mother', from *Forty Nights: Creation centered night prayer* by
Daniel J. McGill. Copyright © 1993 Daniel J. McGill. Used by permission of Paulist Press.
Page 11: 'My God – equally present', from *Psalms of a Laywoman* by Edwina Gateley. Used
by permission of the author.
Page 11: 'Help me to be brave', from *To Barbara with Love* by Joan Bel Geddes. Copyright
© 1974 Holub & Associates. Used by permission.
Page 11: 'Praying a Bible text', from *Jerusalem Prayers for the World Today* by George Appleton.
Copyright © 1974 George Appleton. Used by permission of Miss M. Appleton.
Page 12: 'Jesus, you wasted no time agonizing', from *Turn Over Any Stone* by Edna Hong.
Copyright © 1970 Augsburg Publishing House. Used by permission of Postscript, Inc.
Page 13: 'Some people find the imagination a useful tool', from *Prayer Without Pretending*
by Angela Ashwin. Copyright © 1991 Angela Ashwin. Used by permission.
Page 13: 'I experienced it again today', from *Greater Than Our Hearts: Prayers and reflections*
by Ulrich Schaffer. Copyright © 1981 Ulrich Schaffer. Used by permission of HarperCollins
Publishers.
Page 14: 'Dear God, the pain of this life is more than I can bear', from *Illuminata* by
Marianne Williamson. Copyright © 1994 Marianne Williamson. Used by permission
of Random House.
Page 14: 'Help of the tired ones, I am in need tonight', by Mary Esther Burgoyne from
Moving into a New Now: Faith in the later years by Mildred Tengbom (Minneapolis: Augsburg
Fortress, 1997). Used by permission of Burgoyne's daughter, Ms Ann Holman.
Page 15: 'May the God who listens to our hearts', excerpted from *Swallow's Nest: A feminine
reading of the Psalms* by Marchiene Vroon Rienstra. Copyright © 1992 William B. Eerdmans
Publishing. Used by permission.
Page 15: 'Dear Lord, in the midst of much inner turmoil', from *A Cry for Mercy* by Henri
J.M. Nouwen. Copyright © 1981 Henri J.M. Nouwen. Used by permission of Doubleday,
a division of Bantam Doubleday Dell Publishing Group.
Page 16: 'Almighty God, whose most dear son', from *The Book of Common Prayer* (1979).
Page 16: 'O Lord, it has been a while', from *Your Words in Prayer in Time of Illness* by Father
Arnaldo Pangrazzi. Copyright © 1982 Alba House. Used by permission.
Page 17: 'Thank you, O God, for all the people', Christian Publicity Organization, England.
Used by permission.
Page 17: 'Bless her for not saying', from *Patient Prayers: Talking to God from a hospital bed* by
John V. Chervokas. Copyright © 1989 Crossroads Publishing. Used by permission.
Page 17: 'They don't call. They don't come', from *Right Side Up! Reflections for those living
with serious illness* by Marlene Halpin. Copyright © 1995. Used by permission of Isleswest
Publishing.
Page 18: 'Gently and lightly massage the hands', from *Prayer and Our Bodies* by Flora Slosson
Wuellner. Copyright © 1987 Flora Slosson Wuellner. Used by permission of Upper Room
Books.
Page 19: 'All is ill and very ill', from *Turn Over Any Stone* by Edna Hong. Copyright © 1970
Augsburg Publishing House. Used by permission of Postscript, Inc.
Page 19: 'And so our Good Lord answered', from *Showings* by Julian of Norwich. Translated
by Edmund Colledge and James Walsh. Copyright © 1978 Paulist Press. Used by permission
of Paulist Press.
Page 20: 'That which is impossible for you', from *Showings* by Julian of Norwich. Translated
by Edmund Colledge and James Walsh. Copyright © 1978 Paulist Press. Used by permission
of Paulist Press.
Page 20: 'Once life has almost been taken from you', from *Laughter, Silence and Shouting*.

pray taught by Jesus by Robert B. and Janet B. Ellsworth. Used by permission.

Page 34: 'As swimmers dare', from *Oblique Prayers* by Denise Levertov. Copyright © 1984 Denise Levertov. Used by permission of New Directions Publishing and Laurence Pollinger Limited.

Page 34: 'O Lord, please send me someone', from *Your Words in Prayer in Time of Illness* by Father Arnaldo Pangrazzi. Copyright © 1982 Alba House. Used by permission.

Page 35: 'Dear Lord Jesus, I don't know who I am', Flora Calver. Used by permission of the Reverend Clive Calver, Wheaton, Il.

Page 35: 'Lord of life, send my roots rain', Gerard Manley Hopkins (1844–89).

Page 35: 'You can also pray', from *Love: A fruit always in season* by Mother Teresa, edited by Dorothy S. Hunt (Ignatius Press, 1987).

Page 36: 'When I come to the end of my prayers', from *Survivor Prayers: Talking with God about childhood sexual abuse* by Catherine J. Foote. Copyright © 1994 Catherine J. Foote. Used by permission of Westminster John Knox Press.

Page 38: 'O Lord, whose power to heal', from *Prayers for Today's Church* edited by R.H.L Williams. Copyright © 1977 R.H.L. Williams. Administered and used by permission of Augsburg Fortress.

Page 38: 'Bless your people, Lord', from *National Council of Churches of the Philippines, 14th Biennial Convention Resource Book*, 1989.

Page 39: 'From the mingled light', from *Hoping Against All Hope* by Dom Helder Camara. Original text copyright © 1981 Pendo Verlag AG, Zurich. English translation copyright © Orbis Books. Used by permission of the publishers.

Page 39: 'Lord Jesus Christ, help us not to fall', from *The Hungering Dark* by Frederick Buechner. Copyright © 1969 Frederick Buechner. Used by permission of HarperCollins Publishers.

Page 39: 'All the broken hearts shall rejoice', from *In God's Image*, April 1986. Copyright © Asian Women's Resource Centre. Used by permission.

Page 40: 'I believe that God has the whole world', from *Sharing the Darkness* by Sheila Cassidy. Published and copyright © 1988 Darton, Longman and Todd and 1991 Orbis Books. Used by permission of the publishers.

Page 41: 'God of all good life', from *A Lenten Prayer* by Obie Wright Jr. Copyright © 1994 Personal Papers of Obie Wright Jr, Olney, MD.

Page 41: 'O Lord, once I was smart enough', Lewis B. Smedes from *Peace Prayers*. Copyright © Lewis B. Smedes. Used by permission.

Page 41: 'Lead me from death to life', adapted from the Upanishads.

Page 42: 'Goodness is stronger than evil', from *An African Prayer Book* selected by Desmond Tutu. Copyright © 1995 Desmond Tutu. Reproduced by permission of Hodder and Stoughton Limited and Doubleday, a division of Bantam Doubleday Dell Publishing Group.

Page 42: 'Bless, O God, my enemies with sunshine', from *Forty Nights: Creation centered night prayer* by Daniel J. McGill. Copyright © 1993 Daniel J. McGill. Used by permission of Paulist Press.

Page 43: 'Almighty God and Father of us all', from *Prayer for Pilgrims: A book about ordinary people* by Sheila Cassidy. Copyright © 1980, 1994 HarperCollins Religious Publishers, UK. Used by permission.

Page 43: 'Source of all life, for your name's sake', from *Forty Nights: Creation centered night prayer* by Daniel J. McGill. Copyright ©1993 Daniel J. McGill. Used by permission of Paulist Press.

Page 45: 'Put your ear to the ground', from *Le Desert Est Fertile (The Desert is Fertile)* by Dom Helder Camara. Original text copyright © Desclée de Brouwer, Paris and English translation copyright © 1974 Orbis Books. Used by permission of the publishers.

Page 48: 'I am depressed, O God', from *Psalms of Lament* by Ann Weems. Copyright © 1995 Ann Weems. Used by permission of Westminster John Knox Press.

Page 49: 'How is faith to endure', from *Lament for a Son* by Nicholas Wolterstorff.

Copyright © 1987 William B. Eerdmans Publishing. Used by permission of the publisher.

Page 49: 'I believe in you, O Holy One', from *Woman Witness* by Miriam Therese Winter. Copyright © 1992 Crossroad Publishing Company. Used by permission.

Page 50: 'There's not much to come home to', from *Green Winter* by Elise Maclay. Copyright © 1977 Elise Maclay. Administered and used by permission of Sanford J. Greenburger & Associates.

Page 51: 'O God, hear me! I am tormented', from *Psalms of Lament* by Ann Weems. Copyright © 1995 Ann Weems. Used by permission of Westminster John Knox Press.

Page 52: 'What do I do now with my regrets', from *Lament for a Son* by Nicholas Wolterstorff. Copyright © 1987 William B. Eerdmans Publishing. Used by permission.

Page 53: 'I shall look at the world through tears', from *Lament for a Son* by Nicholas Wolterstorff. Copyright © 1987 William B. Eerdmans Publishing. Used by permission.

Page 53: 'Dear Lord, just as you gave us tear ducts', from *When a Loved One Dies* by Philip W. Williams. Copyright © 1995 Augsburg Fortress. Used by permission.

Page 54: 'Her face thins', from *Contemporary Religious Poetry* edited by Paul Ramsey. Copyright © 1987 Paul Ramsey. Used by permission of Paulist Press.

Page 54: 'Today I read about a man', from *Green Winter* by Elise Maclay. Copyright © 1977 Elise Maclay. Administered and used by permission of Sanford J. Greenburger & Associates.

Page 55: 'O God who brought us to birth', from *Celebrating Women* by H. Ward, J. Wild and J. Morley. Copyright © SPCK 1995 and *Celebrating Women: The new edition*. Copyright © 1995 Janet Morley. Reprinted by permission of Janet Morley and Morehouse Publishing.

Page 55: 'The Lord bless you and keep you', from *When a Loved One Dies* by Philip W. Williams. Copyright © 1995 Augsburg Fortress. Used by permission.

Page 58: 'May God bless us with forgiveness', from *Swallow's Nest: A feminine reading of the Psalms* by Marchiene Vroon Rienstra. Copyright © 1992 William B. Eerdmans Publishing. Used by permission.

Page 58: 'Lord, grant that anger or other bitterness', from *Luther's Works: American edition* edited by Jaroslav Pelikan and Helmut Lehman. Copyright © 1955 Fortress Press and Concordia Publishing House. Used by permission.

Page 58: 'He makes me so damned angry', from *Personal Prayers* by Helen Thomas. Copyright © 1978 Arena Lettres. Used by permission of Ashgate Publishing.

Page 59: 'I cannot forgive', Corrie ten Boom.

Page 59: '_____, I bless you', Marianne Williamson.

Page 59: 'Lord of creation, remind all lovers', from *Lord Be With* by Herbert Brokering. Copyright © Herbert Brokering. Used by permission.

Page 60: 'Our Father in heaven, you gave each', from *Forgiveness is a Work as Well as a Grace* by Edna Hong. Copyright © 1983 Edna Hong. Used by permission of Postscript, Inc.

Page 60: 'The Jesus prayer', from *Jerusalem Prayers for the World Today* by George Appleton. Copyright © 1974 George Appleton. Used by permission of Miss M. Appleton.

Page 61: 'Today, O Lord, I accept', from *Prayers from the Heart* by Richard J. Foster. Copyright © 1994 Richard J. Foster. Used by permission of HarperCollins Publishers.

Page 61: 'Lord Jesus, we are silly sheep', from *Reaching the Heart of Your Teen* by Gary and Anne Marie Ezzo. Copyright © 1997 Gary and Anne Marie Ezzo. Used by permission of Multnomah Publishers.

Page 62: 'The blessing of God whose love reconciles', from *Prayers of Our Hearts: In word and action* by Vienna Cobb Anderson. Copyright © Vienna Cobb Anderson. Used by permission of Crossroad Publishing Company.

Page 64: 'Be silent. Be still', from *There Was No Path So I Trod One* by Edwina Gateley. Copyright © Edwina Gateley. Used by permission of the author.

Page 64: 'My ego is like a fortress', from *Deep as the Hunger* by Howard Thurman (1900–81). Copyright © Howard Thurman. Used by permission of Friends United Press.

Page 65: 'God, teach me to let my soul rest', from *To Barbara With Love* by Joan Bel Geddes. Copyright © Joan Bel Geddes. Administered and used by permission of Holub & Associates.

Page 83: 'May _____ be safe', Buddhist Loving Kindness Prayer.
Page 83: 'Dear Lord, help me to release my need to control', from *Come Apart for Awhile: Exploring four ways to pray taught by Jesus* by Robert B. and Janet B. Ellsworth. Used by permission.
Page 83: 'Life, spilling over the hills', from *Woman Witness* by Miriam Therese Winter. Copyright © 1992 Medical Mission Sisters. Used by permission of Crossroad Publishing.
Page 84: 'May you face life without illusion', from *Autumn Gospel: Women in the second half of life* by Kathleen Fischer. Copyright © 1995 Kathleen Fischer. Used by permission of Paulist Press.
Page 84: 'In the nursing home', from *Otherwise: New and selected poems* by Jane Kenyon. Copyright © 1996 Estate of Jane Kenyon. Used by permission of Graywolf Press, St Paul, MN.
Page 85: 'Oh Lord who took on human flesh', from *A Book of Irish American Blessings and Prayers*. Copyright © 1991 Andrew M. Greeley. Used by permission of Thomas More Publishers.
Page 85: 'Dear Lord, welcome this traveller', from *To Barbara With Love* by Joan Bel Geddes. Copyright © Joan Bel Geddes. Administered and used by permission of Holub & Associates.

Page 88: 'O Lord, Creator, Ruler of the World', from *Morning, Noon and Night* edited by John Carden. Copyright © 1976 Church Missionary Society. Used by permission.
Page 88: 'I suffered, and now there is joy', from *Psalms of a Laywoman* by Edwina Gateley. Copyright © Edwina Gateley. Used by permission.
Page 89: 'For all the good things I do have', from *To Barbara With Love* by Joan Bel Geddes. Copyright © Joan Bel Geddes. Administered and used by permission of Holub & Associates.
Page 90: 'O God, early in the morning I cry', from *Prayers from Prison* by Dietrich Bonhoeffer. Copyright © 1978 Fortress Press. Used by permission.
Page 91: 'I lift up my heart to you in gratitude', from *Prayers for a Planetary Pilgrim* by Edward Hays. Copyright © Forest of Peace Publishing House. Used by permission.
Page 91: 'Today is an ordinary day', from *Survivor Prayers: Talking with God about childhood sexual abuse* by Catherine J. Foote. Copyright © 1994 Catherine J. Foote. Used by permission of Westminster John Knox Press.
Page 92: 'In the godforsaken, obscene quicksand of life', from *Psalms of Lament* by Ann Weems. Copyright © 1995 Ann Weems. Used by permission of Westminster John Knox Press.
Page 92: 'As my mind and heart roam', from *Right Side Up! Reflections for those living with serious illness* by Marlene Halpin. Copyright © 1995 Marlene Halpin. Used by permission of Islewest Publishing.
Page 92: 'It is written', from *A Grateful Heart* by M.J. Ryan. Copyright © 1994 M.J. Ryan. Used by permission of Conari Press.
Page 92: 'We give thanks for our friends', from *The Prayer Tree* by Michael Leunig. Copyright © 1973 Michael Leunig. Used by permission of HarperCollins, Australia.
Page 93: 'To be joyful in the universe is a brave and reckless act', from *A Grateful Heart* by M.J. Ryan. Copyright © 1994 Molly Fumia. Used by permission of Conari Press.
Page 93: 'And in the evening, when I lie in bed', from *The Works of Anne Frank* by Anne Frank. Copyright © 1952, 1959 Otto H. Frank. Used by permission of Doubleday, a division of Bantam Doubleday Dell Publishing Group and the Heinemann Group.
Page 94: 'Lord, I am grateful to you', from *The Little Book of Prayers* by David Schiller. Copyright © 1996 David Schiller. Used by permission of Workman Publishing, New York.

Page 98: 'Hurting, they came to him', from *Kneeling in Jerusalem* by Ann Weems. Copyright © 1992 Oscar Cullman. Used by permission of Westminster John Knox Press.
Page 98: 'Out of the ashes rises the healer', from *Heart of Healing, Heart of Light* by Flora Slosson Wuellner. Copyright © 1992 Flora Slosson Wuellner. Used by permission of Upper Room Books.
Page 99: 'Having eaten my last crumb', from *A Tree Full of Angels* by Macrina Wiederkehr. Copyright © 1988 Macrina Wiederkehr. Used by permission of HarperCollins Publishers.
Page 100: 'Some of you I will hollow out', from *Circle of Mysteries: The women's rosary book* by